THE ITALIAN EXPERIENCE
IN AMERICA

A PICTORIAL HISTORY

THE ITALIAN EXPERIENCE
IN AMERICA

A PICTORIAL HISTORY

REVISED EDITION

MICHAEL D. DEMICHELE

SCRANTON: THE UNIVERSITY OF SCRANTON PRESS

Library of Congress Cataloging-in-Publication Data

DeMichele, Michael D.
    The Italian experience in America : a pictorial history / by Michael DeMichele.--2nd ed.
        p. cm.
    Includes bibliographical references and index.
    ISBN 1-58966-105-2
    1. Italian Americans--History. 2. Italian Americans--History--Pictorial works. I. Title.

E184.I8D35 2004

973'.0451--dc22   2004059569

Distribution:

The University of Scranton Press
445 Madison Avenue
Scranton   PA   18510
Phone: 1–800–941–3081
Fax: 1–800–941–8804

Book Design by
Trinka Ravaioli Pettinato, Grapevine Design

PRINTED IN THE UNITED STATES OF AMERICA

TO MY FRIEND AND COLLEAGUE

JOHN L. EARL III, PH.D.

1933–1996

CONTENTS

ACKNOWLEDGMENTS

I wish to acknowledge and express my sincere appreciation to The University of Scranton for granting me a sabbatical leave which enabled me to research and write this second edition of my pictorial history. I remain indebted to all those individuals in various ways in preparing my first edition, particularly Fred Rotondaro, Executive Director of the National Italian-American Foundation; Leroy Bellamy of the Prints and Photography Division of the Library of Congress; Mr. Gunter Pohl of the Local History and Genealogy Division of the New York Public Library; Robert Lazar, Archivist of the ILGWU Archives; Ed Rogers of *The Scranton Times*; Cathy Butsko of the Museum of the City of New York; Mark Hirschfeld, TAT Communications Company; Diana Zimmerman of the Center for Migration Studies; Laura V. Monti of the Boston Public Library; Patricia Akre of the San Francisco Public Library; Ted J. LoCascio of Standard Brands; Henry A. Sandbach of the Del Monte Corporation; Richard M. Buck of the Library and Museum of the Performing Arts; Tom Powell of *WDAU*-TV in Scranton; Dominic Candeloro of the American-Italian Historical Association; Charles J. Polzer, S.J. of the Southwestern Mission Research Center; Robert Connolly of the Casa Italiana of Columbia University; Thomas L. Scott, S.J.; Thomas A. McGoff; John L. Earl III and Kevin Norris of The University of Scranton. In this second edition I'm most grateful to all those individuals who have helped me to revise and update my work, especially John Marino, Manager of Research and Cultural Affairs of the National Italian-American Foundation; Dona DeSanctis, Deputy Executive Director of the Order Sons of Italy of America; Barbara Peirano, Executive Administrator of UNICO National; Dawn Leikness of Wire Image; Joseph Matalone, Director of Development of the National Italian-American Sports Hall of Fame; the staff of the Prints and Photograph Division of the Library of Congress; Chris Yarem, Photo Lab Supervisor at CVS; the numerous celebrities from all fields who gave permission to reproduce their photos; and my colleagues at The University of Scranton, Roy P. Domenico, Robert A. Spalletta and Carol Long. I'm also obliged to thank two of my student research assistants, Rachel Pike and Tiffany Fazio; Jane A. Wesloski, who assisted me greatly with my correspondence and typed parts of this manuscript, deserves special praise. Finally, I should like to express my deepest gratitude to my wife, Rosemary, who continually encouraged me in the undertaking of this project.

PREFACE

In 1982 after extensive research in the photography archives of the Library of Congress, the Archives of the United States, the New York Public Library, and numerous other photography archives, I published the first edition of *The Italian Experience in America: A Pictorial History*. With a concise, informative text and more than 220 images, I hope that my book gave a better understanding of Italians in American history than would have been possible from an unillustrated work. While scholars and avid readers no doubt would have recognized some of the photographs used as illustrations in other works, I feel I was able to bring to light other original photographs to be viewed for the first time.

It is now more than two decades since my book's debut. Much has happened in the Italian-American community in that time. Both my colleagues at The University of Scranton and my many friends in the Italian-American community have suggested that I undertake a revision of my first edition, especially those chapters dealing with Italian-American contributions in politics, economics, the humanities, and the social sciences, as well as the arts, sports, and entertainment.

On sabbatical from my teaching duties at The University of Scranton I was able to revisit a number of great libraries, historical societies, and museums that have large depositories of photographs of Italian-Americans. I found those photograph selections much better catalogued today and much more accessible to scholars. I was able to do extensive readings of historical articles, books, and other monographs on Italian-Americans that have been written in the two decades since my first edition was published. With advances in technology, especially the evolution of the Internet, I was able to correspond more easily with Italian-American societies, foundations, and organizations, as well as politicians, people in the business world, athletes, entertainers, and other celebrities in order to obtain their photographs.

In this second edition it is my goal to incorporate some of the findings of the scholarship published in the 1980s and 1990s and to add new photographs while deleting a number of old photographs in order to bring the story of the Italian experience in America up-to-date.

As with the first edition I hope that my illustrated history of the Italian experience in America will not only complement the work of scholars, but will also give a more vivid understanding of Italian-American history than readers would get from an unillustrated work. While the avid reader will no doubt recognize that some of the photographs used as illustrations in this volume have appeared in dozens of other books, there are many other photographs never published before. In preparing this work for publication I have come to realize that it is impossible to cover every subject connected with the Italian experience in America, especially in the space of a pictorial book. I have tried, therefore, to be selective. While I have sincerely attempted to do my utmost to allocate appropriate words and illustrations to events, places, and individuals, I am sure that my judgment is not without fault. I particularly wish to point out that the citation of prominent individuals featured in this book should in no way be construed as suggestive that other renowned individuals not appearing in this work are less important in their respective fields of endeavor.

Christopher Columbus
leaving Palos, Spain by
the artist Joaquin Y.
Bastida. (Courtesy of the
Mariners Museum,
Newport News, Virginia)

CHAPTER ONE

THE FIRST ITALIANS

From the discovery of the New World in the fifteenth century to the present, Italians and Italian-Americans have continued to play a vital role in the social, political, economic, and cultural history of America. Christopher Columbus was, of course, the first of the four great early Italian explorers of America. This remarkable adventurer grew up in the bustling Mediterranean seaport town of Genoa where he came to know ships, the Indies' sailors, chartmakers, navigators, traders, and explorers. While only in his teens, he sailed in numerous vessels that visited the ports along the Mediterranean Coast. His first venture out on the Atlantic resulted in his being shipwrecked off the coast of Portugal. He settled for a time in Lisbon where he found work as a chartmaker, studying mathematics, astronomy, and Latin, and also learning about shipbuilding, rigging, and the latest navigation instruments. He extensively read books on philosophy, geography, and exploration, which encouraged his preoccupation with finding a new route to the Indies.

Columbus came to believe that he could reach the Indies by sailing directly west. Just how he developed this theory remains a mystery, but it is believed that he was deeply influenced by learned physician and geographer Paolo Tascanelli of Florence, who believed that if Marco Polo's estimate of the size of Asia was correct, it would be feasible to reach it by sailing less than 3,000 miles west of Spain. Had Columbus known that the actual distance was more than 10,000 miles west of Spain, he probably would not have undertaken his voyage because the established route to the wealth of the Indies was much shorter. If he had known that the American continent lay in his path he probably would not have undertaken the journey since he really sought a new route to an old world rather than the discovery of a new world. Having failed to gain financial support for his epic voyage from King John II of Portugal, he turned to the Spanish court of Ferdinand and Isabella for assistance. Eventually, he convinced Isabella to finance his venture. He set sail for Asia on August 3, 1492, from

Palos, Spain, with three small ships. Because these islands were supposed to be at the latitude of Japan, he sailed by way of the Canary Islands to take on added provisions. For more than a month Columbus and his crew had no sight of land. Then on October 12, 1492, they sighted land. It proved to be what is known as Watling Island in the Bahamas. Convinced that he had discovered a new westward sea route to the Indies, he made three more voyages to the New World, never realizing he had not reached Asia. He had, however, made the discovery of a new continent, which would prove of far greater consequence than his originally intended goal of finding a new route to Asia.

Columbus' lead ship, *The Santa Maria* **from a painting by Harry Ogden. (Courtesy of the New York Historical Society)**

News of Columbus's discoveries encouraged other navigators to cross the Atlantic to discover new trade routes. Among these was a Venetian, Giovanni Caboto, who changed his name to John Cabot when he emigrated to England. Like Columbus, Cabot sought a new route to the Indies. Cabot was able to convince Henry VII of England to grant him letters patent to raise the necessary money for his enterprise. Around the end of May 1497, with one vessel, the *Matthew*, he and his crew of fifty men sailed from Bristol, England, in search of the spices and treasures of the Indies. He too failed to discover what he sought. Instead, he reached the coast of America near Newfoundland, and became the first explorer to look upon the American mainland. Cabot, moreover, believed that he had landed on the coast of Asia, and that by sailing inland he would reach its rich cities and inhabitants. Shortages of food and provisions prevented Cabot from exploring the interior, and he returned to England. He undertook a second voyage in 1498, but details are unavailable. Cabot's voyages provided the basis for the English claim to North America and resulted in the discovery of the rich fishing off the coast of Newfoundland.

In 1499 Amerigo Vespucci, a Venetian in the service of Spain, set out on an expedition that followed directly in the track of Columbus. Accompanied by Juan de

Landing of Columbus
in the West Indies,
October 12th, 1492.
(Courtesy of the
Architect of the
U.S. Capitol)

la Cosa, a former pilot of Columbus, and using Columbus's charts and calculations, Vespucci reached the northeastern coast of South America on the easternmost bulge of Brazil. During the next four years, he made two other voyages during which he surveyed the coast of Brazil south of its easternmost point, to the mouth of the La Plata River. When he returned to Europe in 1504, he wrote several letters to his benefactors in which he told of his journey, making it very clear that neither he nor Columbus had explored the "Indies," but instead had discovered a *Mundus Novus* (or New World.) These accounts fell into the hands of the German scholar Martin Waldseemüller, who, although giving credit to Columbus for discovering the islands of the Caribbean, proposed that the continental landmass be called America after Amerigo Vespucci—the man who realized that this land beyond the Atlantic was not the "Indies" but a "New World." No other man has ever had such a monument as two continents named after him.

Engraving of Giovanni
da Verrazano.
(Courtesy of the
Library of Congress)

The last of the four great early Italian explorers was the Florentine Giovanni da Verrazano, whom Francis I of France sent in 1524 to discover a westward route to China and the Spice Islands.

Left: Portrait of Amerigo Vespucci by Constantino Brumidi. (Courtesy of the Architect of the U.S. Capitol)

John Cabot's discovery of North America. (Courtesy of the Library of Congress)

On January 17, 1524, Verrazano, with his ship *La Dauphine* and a crew of fifty men, left the coast of France. Crossing the frigid Atlantic in mid-winter, he reached what is now called Cape Fear of the North Carolina coast on March 1, 1524. From there he proceeded to explore the North American coast from Cape Hatteras to Maine. At one point, he sailed inland into New York Bay where he anchored his ship and explored the interior. Not only did this make him the first European to enter New York Harbor, but it also made him the first to give descriptions of the American mainland. During the next several years he made at least two more crossings of the Atlantic from Europe. He did not return from the voyage he made from France in 1529. While Verrazano's ship *La Flamengue* anchored off the shore of Guadeloupe in the Bahamas, he waded ashore. Struck from behind by Carib Indians, he was killed, roasted, and eaten by the natives, making Verrazano the first Italian meal consumed in America.

Equestrian Statue of Father Eusebio Kino on horseback. (Courtesy of Charles W. Polzer, S.J.)

Besides these four Italian discoverers of America, other Italians played an important role in the early history of the New World. Some of these Italians came as soldiers and adventurers while others came as missionaries. One of the most enterprising of these individuals was the Franciscian missionary Marco da Nizza, a native of Savoy who, in the service of Spain, explored the Spanish colonial empire of Mexico in 1538 searching for the legendary seven cities of Cibola. He also traveled north through Arizona and New Mexico of which he related tales of fabulous riches—an interesting if inaccurate account of the Spanish Southwest. Another such venturesome man of God was the Jesuit priest Eusebio Kino, who was born in the Tyrol in the northern part of Italy. Kino, together with another Jesuit priest, explored and mapped nearly all of the Spanish southwest colonial frontier, proving that southern California was not an island but a peninsula. Father Kino also established no fewer than nineteen Spanish missions in California before he died in 1711. Meanwhile, the Jesuit priest Francesco Bresanni brought the

The Griffin, which was constructed by Enrico di Tonti, entering the harbor at Mackinaw. (Courtesy of the National Gallery of Art)

word of Christianity to the Iroquois Indians in the territory of New York, and became the first man to explore and pen a description of Niagara Falls.

Accompanying the great French explorer, Robert La Salle, in the Mississippi Valley in 1678, was the debonair Neapolitan soldier of fortune, Enrico Di Tonti (or Henri De Tonty as the French preferred to call him). Prior to his coming to America, Tonti served as a naval officer in the French service. During the Sicilian Wars between France and Spain, Tonti's right hand was blown off by a grenade, after which he came to be known as "the man with the iron claw." La Salle and Tonti explored the Great Lakes, and Tonti built and sailed the *Griffin*, the first large ship on the Great Lakes. Tonti also founded the first white settlement in Illinois, built Fort St. Louis in Texas, and after La Salle's death, founded the first French settlement in Arkansas at the juncture of the Mississippi and Arkansas Rivers.

While some Italian settlers came as individuals, others came as groups. The Jamestown settlement saw the arrival of several Italians in 1610, brought over to plant vineyards and produce wine. Another group of Italians from Venetia were brought to Jamestown in 1622 to try to develop the art of glassmaking. The Dutch recruited nearly 300 Waldensians from Piedmont to settle in what is now New Castle, Delaware. At the same time, Italian Catholics settled in Maryland, while others were recruited to raise cotton in Georgia. From the sixteenth century on, Italian settlers served as soldiers and missionaries in Florida. By 1720 an Italian colony had developed in Louisiana. For the most part, these Italians integrated themselves into the American colonies as farmers, craftsmen, fishermen, missionaries, and political figures.

The most influential Italian political figure to come to America in the period of the American Revolution was Filippo Mazzei, a Tuscan physician, agronomist, and philosopher. Invited by Thomas Jefferson to found an experimental farm in Virginia whereby the agricultural production of that colony might be increased, Mazzei arrived in Virginia in 1773 with a party of Italian farm workers. He soon became involved, however, in the American struggle for independence. From 1774 to 1781 he wrote a series of articles and pamphlets in which he continually pronounced that equality must be the basis of American democracy and that independence from England was the only true course for Americans to follow. Evidently Thomas Jefferson was deeply influenced by Mazzei,

Bas-relief of Enrico di Tonti, Marquette Building, Chicago. (Courtesy of Illinois State Historical Society)

The ruin of Cocospora which was one of Father Eusebio Kino's missions. (Courtesy of Charles W. Polzer, S.J.)

Bust of Philip Mazzei in solid bronze, sculptured by Joseph Amelio Finelli. (Courtesy of the National Italian-American Foundation)

particularly by his pronouncement that "All men are by nature equally free and independent." In 1779 the Governor of Virginia, Patrick Henry, commissioned Mazzei to secure a loan from Peter Leopold, the Grand Duke of Tuscany, for the purpose of supporting the American War of Independence. Although unsuccessful in obtaining the desired funds, Mazzei convinced the Grand Duke to make a formal statement giving his personal support to the American cause. This statement encouraged a number of Italians in the colonies to enlist in the American Continental Army. At the completion of the Revolutionary War, Mazzei sought a position of political prominence in Virginia. Disappointed that he received no such reward, he returned to Italy in 1785 where he spent his remaining years. While in Italy he continued his correspondence with Jefferson and was responsible for sending a number of excellent Italian sculptors and painters to America with the purpose of building and decorating the new Capital Building in Washington, D.C. He died in 1816.

One of the most noteworthy Italian heroes of the American Revolution was Giuseppe Maria Francesco Vigo, a native of Mondovì in Piedmont. As a young man he

Colonel Francis Vigo. (Courtesy of Indiana State Library)

served as a soldier in the Spanish Army, first in Cuba and later in New Orleans. While in America, he resigned his commission in the Spanish Army and became a fur trader and explorer in the Old Northwest Territory. When the American Revolution broke out, he decided to join George Rogers Clark, who commanded the American Continental Army in the West against the British. Vigo not only made a substantial military contribution, but he also made a financial one to Clark's forces. This assistance enabled the American forces to defeat the British at Vincennes in 1779, thus giving the colonials virtual control of the northwestern regions of the Mississippi Valley.

Among the many other Italians who served the cause of American independence were William Paca, Governor of the colony of Maryland and a signer of the Declaration of Independence; Major Cosimo Medici, who fought with the North Carolina Light Dragoons at the Battle of Brandywine; Vincenzo Rossi, who fought under Patrick Henry in the Virginia Militia; Colonel Richard Taliaferro, who was killed at the Battle of Guilford Hall; William Peyrounie, who captained the Virginia Regiment at Fort Duquesne; and Christopher Baldi, who served as a captain in the Continental Army and was promoted to the rank of brigadier general after the war.

Italians also made their mark in other fields in the colonial and postcolonial periods following the Revolutionary War. As early as 1757 colonials applauded Giovanni Palma, who gave one of the first musical concerts in America. Giovanni Gualdo not only gave concerts and composed music, but he also opened a school of music in Philadelphia in 1767. Other Italian soloists, harpsicordists, violinists, and pianists toured the American colonies from Rhode Island to South Carolina. In 1799 Filippo Traetta, a composer from Venetia, founded the first conservatory of music in the United States. During the last decade of the eighteenth century, the first Italian operas were produced in America and performed in such cities as Baltimore, New York, Philadelphia, and New Orleans. The man most responsible for the success of the Italian opera in America was Lorenzo Da Ponte, Mozart's former librettist, who arrived in America in 1805. Over the next three decades, Da Ponte tirelessly promoted the importing of Italian opera companies to America. Through his enterprise, the first Italian opera house in America was built in New York City in 1833.

William Paca. (Courtesy of the Library of Congress)

Lorenzo Da Ponte. (Courtesy of the New York Public Library at Lincoln Center)

A portrait of Carlo Franzoni by Pietro Bonanni.
(Courtesy of the Architect of the U.S. Capitol)

Constantino Brumidi, the "Michelangelo" of the United States Capitol. (Courtesy of the Architect of the U.S. Capitol)

"Discovery of America" by Luigi Persico, originally located at the East Front of the U.S. Capitol, but transferred in 1976 to the Smithsonian Institution. (Courtesy of the Architect of the U.S. Capitol)

Although very few Italian sculptors and painters came to America prior to the Civil War, Italian influence on American art was profound during the early years of the republic. Giuseppe Ceracchi, a Roman artist who arrived in America in 1791, was responsible for sculpting magnificent live-size busts of Washington, Jefferson, Hamilton, and many of other founding fathers. Giovanni Andrei, Giuseppe and Carlo Fronzoni, Antonio Capellano, Giuseppe Valperta, and Luigi Persico were among the numerous Italian artists commissioned by the U. S. government to adorn the Capitol with their sculptures. The government also hired Constantino Brumidi, a noted fresco painter and political exile who came from Rome in 1852, to decorate the Capitol with his paintings. Brumidi worked more than a quarter century painting frescoes through-out the building. His "Cincinnatus at the Plough" and "Surrender of Conwallis" are reputed to be the first true frescoes painted in the United States. His brilliant "Apotheosis of Washington," which covers more than 4,500 square feet of the concave

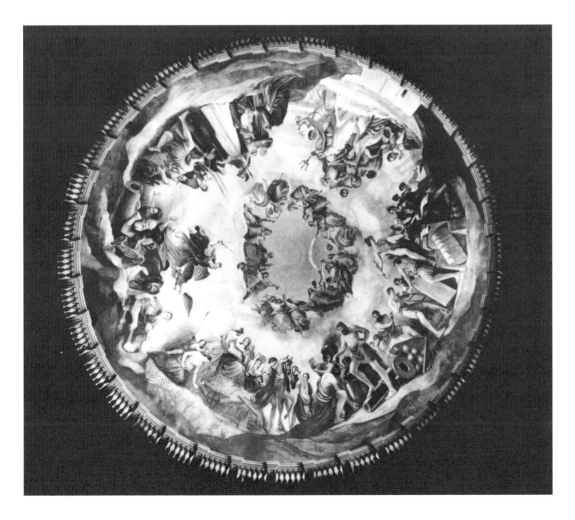

The "Apotheosis of Washington" by Constantino Brumidi in the Dome of the U.S. Capitol. (Courtesy of the Architect of the U.S. Capitol)

Above: "Car of History" (clock) by Carlo Franzoni, a Marble statue of Clio over-looking Statuary Hall in the U.S. Capitol. (Courtesy of the Architect of the U.S. Capitol)

Right: George Washington in consultation with Thomas Jefferson and Alexander Hamilton by Constantino Brumidi in the Senate Wing of the U.S. Capitol. (Courtesy of the Architect of the U.S. Capitol)

surface of the dome was executed by Brumidi in less than one year. The only reward this dedicated artist ever desired was that he ". . . may live long enough to make beautiful the Capitol of the one country on earth in which there is liberty." Unfortunately, he died in 1877 while still working on a monumental fresco depicting major scenes of American history on the rotunda frieze. In addition to Brumidi, Michele Felice Cone and Giuseppe Fragnani had considerable influence on American painting during these formative years. Both Cone and Fragnani presage the American school of art by portraying distinctly American subjects in their paintings, rather than reminding America of its European cultural heritage as Brumidi so often did in his art.

Less famous, but no less significant, were the numerous Italian painters and musicians who contributed to the development of the entertainment industry of America. Designing sets, painting scenes, and playing musical instruments in orches-

Cornwallis sues for cessation of hostilities under the flag of truce by Constantino Brumidi in the Members' Private Dining Room in the U.S. Capitol. (Courtesy of the Architect of the U.S. Capitol)

Antonio Meucci, who had constructed a primitive version of the telephone twenty-six years before Alexander Graham Bell. (Courtesy of the Smithsonian Institution)

Father Giovanni Grazzi, S.J. (Courtesy of Georgetown University)

tras for operas and theatrical works, these artists made stage performances come alive. In the field of education Carlo Bellini, Lorenzo Da Ponte, Pietro Bachi, and Vincenzo Botto became professors at leading American universities, while Father Giovanni Grassi, an Italian Jesuit, became president of Georgetown College in Washington, D.C. in 1812—the first Catholic institution of higher learning in America. A few Italians also made their mark in science. For example, Antonio Meucci, who came to America in 1845, invented a primitive form of the telephone nearly twenty-six years before Alexander Graham Bell exhibited his invention at the Philadelphia exposition.

Official immigration records indicated that fewer than 14,000 Italian immigrants had entered this country by the outbreak of the Civil War in 1861. Most of those had come from northern provinces in Italy such as Lombardy, Venetia, Piedmont, and Tuscany. Although they settled in nearly every state in the country, California, New York, and Pennsylvania boasted the largest Italian populations. Massachusetts, Connecticut, Rhode Island, Maryland, Georgia, Louisiana, Missouri, and Minne-sota had recognizable Italian communities. These Italians worked as farmers, fishermen, miners, teachers, entertainers, craftsmen, businessmen, and professionals. They blended economically and socially with non-Italian immigrants as well as with native-born Americans. A few gained wealth and fame, but most had to work and struggle very hard to survive in their newly adopted land. In the decades preceding the Civil War, America was also home to a

Camp of the Garibaldi Guard. (From *Leslie's Illustrated History of the Civil War*, 1896)

number of Italian political exiles, such as Giuseppe Garibaldi, who later returned to Italy to champion the cause of national unification.

Despite the relatively small population of Italians in America at the time of the Civil War, more than two hundred served as officers in both the Union and Confederate Armies. Taking up arms for the Union, Italian-Americans formed a regiment known as the Garibaldi Guard. This regiment distinguished itself throughout the war, particularly at the Battle of Gettysburg, where it suffered fifteen dead and eighty wounded. Four Italians attained the rank of general in the Union forces. They were Luigi Palma di Cesnola, Enrico Fardella, Francis Spinola, and Eduardo Ferrero—the only general to command an all black combat division during the war. Three Italians in the Union army, Giuseppe Sova, Orlando Caruna, and Luigi Palma di Cesnola, were awarded the Congressional Medal of Honor. After the war, Cesnola would become U. S. consul to Cyprus, and in 1879 would be appointed the first director of the Metropolitan Museum of Art in New York. Fighting for the South were five hundred Italians serving in Louisiana's European Brigade and dozens more in the Mississippi cavalry and Alabama infantry. Decimus et Ultimus Barziza, a

Guiseppe Garibaldi, whom President Lincoln offered a Major General's commission in the Union Army. (Courtesy of the Library of Congress)

Confederate officer in Hood's Texas Brigade, led his men with great daring in a half-dozen battles from Malvern Hill to Gettysburg. Wounded at the Battle of Gettysburg, he was captured by the Union soldiers. He escaped his captors by jumping from a prison train as it sped through the Pennsylvania countryside. A year after the war, he settled in Texas where he practiced law and served for two terms for the state legislature.

During the decade and a half following the Civil War, approximately

Luigi Palma di Cesnola. (Courtesy of the Metropolitan Museum of Art)

General Edward Ferrero. (Courtesy of the Library of Congress)

60,000 Italians, mainly from southern Italy, immigrated to America. Most of these immigrants were poor, unskilled laborers who found their experience in America at this time a particularly harsh ordeal. Unscrupulous captains of industry, insensitive political leaders, and economic depression in the 1870s made life miserable not only for immigrants, but also for significant numbers of native-born Americans. Unable to find employment in this country, many Italians returned to Italy. Where employment was available, Italians often found themselves competing for those jobs with other

Decimus et Ultimus Barziza, a Confederate Officer in Hood's Texas Brigade, who later became one of the greatest criminal lawyers in Texas history. He was also twice elected to the Texas State Legislature. (Courtesy of the Texas State Archives)

immigrants and native-born Americans. In industrial towns and coal mining areas, employers often used Italians as strikebreakers. Italians soon found themselves caught up in the development of the labor movement in this nation. Less-fortunate Italians who were unable to escape back to Italy or find employment sought refuge in large tenement slums such as those found in Lower Manhattan in New York City. By 1880, Italian immigration to America began to develop a pattern that would continue for the next four decades.

CHAPTER TWO

MASS MIGRATION AND SETTLEMENT

Nearly four million Italians immigrated to America between 1880 and 1920. Unlike the earlier Italians who came to America from the northern provinces of Lombardy, Venetia, Tuscany, Umbria, and Piedmont, this new wave of immigrants came mainly from the southern Italian provinces of Apulia, Abruzzi, Calabria, Basilicata, and Sicily. Southern Italy and its inhabitants differed significantly from the area and inhabitants of the North. Whereas a substantial number of northern Italians spoke the Florentine dialect of Tuscany, the southern Italians were apt to speak various village or regional dialects. Illiteracy also was more common in the South. Northern Italians tended to be taller, huskier, and lighter complexioned than their countrymen in the South. On the one hand, the Po River, an abundant rainfall, proper irrigation, and good farming methods made the farmlands of Piedmont, Lombardy, and

The beautifully scenic but harsh land of the *Mezzogiorno.* (Courtesy of the Italian State Tourist Office)

19

Hard times in the
Mezzogiorno.
(Courtesy of
ILGWU Archives)

Venetia the richest in Italy. On the other hand, the lack of a natural water supply, an unpredictable rainfall, deforestation practices, and failure to create an artificial irrigation system created a very arid soil and poor farming conditions in the South. While the North began to industrialize in the nineteenth century, the South remained in a feudal-agrarian state, and the southern Italian peasant (or *contadini*) continued to live in poverty and squalor. The South came to be called the *Mezzogiorno* and was thought of as "the land that time forgot."

The unification of Italy in 1861 brought rapid industrialization and prosperity to the North. It did not, however, bring the much-expected relief to the southern Italian peasants. The condition of the *contadini* did not improve. In fact, their plight grew worse. They soon found themselves dominated by absentee northern landlords who charged high rents and paid low wages. The new northern-dominated national government in Rome paid more attention to maintaining itself in power than to the problems of the ordinary citizen. Huge expenditures connected with the bureaucratic administration of a united Italy meant higher taxes and greater debts for the *contadini*. Local graft and corruption among public officials in the provinces of the South further exacerbated the situation. Even more tragic than the political disorder were the natural disasters that struck the *Mezzogiorno* particularly hard in the last quarter of the nineteenth century. Cases of malaria and cholera reached almost epidemic proportions in the 1880s. Phylloxera, a dreaded plant parasite, devastated the vineyards of the South during the 1890s. At the same time the decline of the sulphur trade in Sicily caused further unemployment and hardship. Primitive agricultural methods and nonarable soil caused southern Italy's agricultural production to fall far behind that of the North. This caused economic depression and still further lowered the standard of living for southern Italians. Soil conditions in Abruzzi were so bad that the *contadini* often awoke before sunrise and walked long distances from their villages to find a farm plot that would grow crops. For all their efforts, the *contadini* barely had enough food to sustain him-self and his family. Too often meals consisted of only a bit of bread dipped in oil and salt. In spite of despotic oppression, natural disasters, and economic depression, the population of southern Italy increased at an alarming rate. This pressure of overpopu-lation upon the means of subsistence made life in the *Mezzogiorno* intolerable.

As oppression and depression lingered in southern Italy, news of opportunities in America spread to the most remote villages of the *Mezzogiorno*. American industri-al recruiters, steamship agents, and labor contractors (or *padroni*) boasted to the *con-tadini* about the freedom, opportunities for work, wealth, and prosperity in the United States. These stories proved irresistible to the poor southern Italian peasants, who grew to see America as the only hope for escaping the poverty and despair of their native land. So the *contadini* sold their crops, farm plots, and livestock, or they borrowed money, to pay for their passage to America. Although some had intended to leave the *Mezzogiorno* forever, many had intended to earn enough money in America to return home and lead a more comfortable life. Nonetheless, from 1880 to 1900 the number of Italian immigrants to America reached nearly 1,000,000, and during the next decade it

Primitive agricultural methods employed by farmers in southern Italy. (Courtesy of the Italians in Chicago Project funded by an NEH grant)

The *Imperator* leaves New York Harbor after depositing cargo of immigrants at Ellis Island in 1913. (Courtesy of the Library of Congress)

totaled 2,945,877. In the peak year of 1907 it reached 285,731. During and immediately after World War I, the rate of Italian immigration to America dropped significantly. However, more than 200,000 Italians managed to enter America in 1921, just before the passage of the immigrant restriction legislation by the U. S. Congress.

Several European shipping lines provided the immigrant with steamship service from various Mediterranean ports to New York and Boston. Nearly ninety percent of the emigrants from Italy came in steerage, which was the least expensive passenger section of the ship. Crossing the Atlantic in steerage was an anguishing experience. Immigrants found themselves with little more than a lumpy mattress in a narrow row of double-decker beds in an overcrowded and ill-ventilated area that was usually below the water line. The rancid food, body stench, and smell of vomit from seasick passengers, in addition to maltreatment by the crew, made the voyage, which usually took from ten to fifteen days, seem like an eternity.

Italian immigrants "just off the boat" en route to be processed at Ellis Island. (Courtesy of the Library of Congress)

Immigrants crowd the deck of the
***S.S. Patricia* in 1906 as they prepare**
to disembark at Ellis Island.
(Courtesy of the Library of Congress)

The first point of disembarkation for the vast majority of steerage passengers was Ellis Island in New York Harbor. During the peak years of immigration (1880–1920), these newcomers often waited for hours on barges before they were set ashore on the pier opposite the main entrance of Ellis Island.

U.S. Inspectors examining the eyes of immigrants at Ellis Island. (Courtesy of the Library of Congress)

From there, they were directed to climb stairs on the east side of the Great Hall and then moved through a maze of corridors where they were given a medical examination to check for contagious diseases, physical defects, and obvious mental disorders. Meanwhile, another team of doctors also gave often more through medical examinations including checking the eyes for glaucoma. Those who passed these examinations were herded to the registry section in the Great Hall where they were questioned by another group of inspectors. There, examiners wanted to make sure that the ship's manifest was accurate and that immigrants were not involved in contract labor—a practice outlawed by the U. S. government since 1885. The questioning of immigrants was done through an interpreter and usually involved about twenty questions. Immigrants who aroused the suspicions of the inspectors were detained, and some were ultimately deported. However, nearly ninety-five percent were approved for entry and given their "admitted" ticket to America.

The Registry Hall at Ellis Island where immigrants were herded like cattle through a series of inspections that would determine whether they would enter the U.S. (Courtesy of the Library of Congress)

Italian family on the small boat of the U.S. Immigration Service which carried them from the pier to Ellis Island. (Photo by Lewis W. Hine— Courtesy of the New York Public Library)

Below: Aerial view of Ellis Island taken in 1921. (Courtesy of the National Park Service)

A newly arrived Italian immigrant family show expressions of mixed emotions as they are about to enter their newly adopted land. (Courtesy of the Library of Congress)

Above: Italian immigrants waiting to recover their lost baggage at Ellis Island. (Photo by Lewis W. Hine—Courtesy of the New York Public Library)

Left: Group of Italians in the Railroad Waiting Room at Ellis Island. (Photo by Lewis W. Hine—Courtesy of the New York Public Library)

Guide books given to Italian immigrants at Ellis Island urged them to go to southern and western states to farm, yet the vast majority settled in the northeastern cities of New York, Pennsylvania, New Jersey, Rhode Island, Connecticut, and Massachusetts. They sought the company of their *paesani* (or countrymen) who came from their same province and spoke their same dialect. "Little Italies," as they came to

The Mulberry Bend about 1888-89. (Photo by Jacob A. Riis—Courtesy of the Museum of the City of New York)

Rear tenement in Italian section of New York City. (Photo by Jacob A. Riis—Courtesy of the Museum of the City of New York)

be called, sprang up in every major city in the northeastern United States. New York City had an Italian population of nearly half a million by 1920, while Philadelphia and Boston had Italian immigrant populations close to one hundred thousand. Chicago, New Orleans, Cleveland, St. Louis, and San Francisco were the only noneastern cities to attract substantial numbers of Italian immigrants. Scattered groups, however, settled in nearly every state in the country and labored in almost every occupation.

The prototype for other "Little Italies" in the United States, New York's "Little Italy" grew in the Lower East Side of Manhattan. Clustered on and around Mulberry Street were Italian grocery stores, fruit markets, restaurants, bakeries, butcher shops, barber shops, banks, and a host of other businesses operated by Italians. Dense populations and slum living characterized most of the "Little Italies" in the United States. The overwhelming majority of the inhabitants of the community lived in four- or five-story brick tenement houses previously inhabited by earlier immigrant groups. These rundown buildings were dirty, damp, dark, and freezing in the winter and sweltering in the summer. They lacked proper ventilation, bathrooms, and hot water. As many as three hundred inhabitants were crammed into each of these multistory firetraps. A family of six or seven might have lived in one small room. The yards and alleys behind these dwellings were filthy and strewn with garbage, violating every sort of sanitary code. Such conditions bred rats, insects, and disease. One block on Mulberry Street was called "lung block" because so many residents on that block had died of tuberculosis.

Italian immigrants spent their first years in such slum neighborhoods not by choice, but by necessity. Often poor, illiterate, and unskilled, they worked twelve to sixteen hours a day to meet living expenses. It took exceptional economy to save and uncommon energy to find time to earn enough money to make a rapid exit from slum life. Had it not been for the closeness of the tight-knit Italian family and the familiar surroundings of one's own *paesani*, life for the immigrant would have been intolerable. "Little Italies" everywhere became the permanent home for some Italian immigrants, but most were determined not to live out their years in those ghettos. And, eventually, most of them left.

Teaming streets of the heart of New York's "Little Italy." (Courtesy of the Library of Congress)

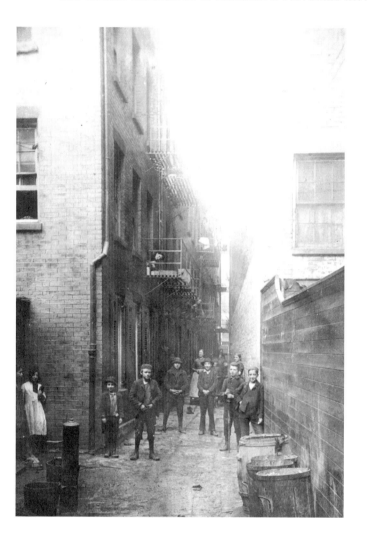

A children's playground in Mullen's Alley near Mulberry Street. (Photo by Jacob A. Riis—Courtesy of the Library of Congress)

As in New York City, Italian immigrants followed a similar pattern of settlement and were offered the same dismal slum conditions in Boston, Philadelphia, Pittsburgh, Baltimore, Chicago, St. Louis, and Cleveland. Even in the Little Italy of San Francisco, which had a large population of northern Italian immigrants, and in New Orleans, which had a long-established southern Italian community, the basic mode of Italian settlement was much the same as in other big cities.

Despite the many hardships endured by the Italian newcomers, life for them in America was not merely one of continual misery. Life in the New World for the immigrant also meant excitement, adventure, freedom from oppression, and the belief that ambition, hard work, and perseverance would bring a better future. The streets of the Little Italies throbbed with the life and promises of the New World, tempered, of course, by the familiar smells, sounds, and customs of the Old World.

In the early twentieth century, mutual-aid societies and fraternal organizations, usually founded by Italians who had immigrated earlier, helped new immigrants with their most pressing problems. Associations such as the Society for Italian Immigrants, the Society for Italian Unity and Fraternity, the Italian Mutual Aid Society, the Italian-American Alliance, the Italian-American Civic Union, and the National Order of the Sons of Italy were among the more prominent groups. They provided financial, med-

Italian lodgers in
Bayard Street
Tenement about
1889. (Photo by
Jacob A. Riis—
Courtesy of the
Museum of the
City of New York)

Child of the tenements.
(Photo by Jacob A. Riis—
Courtesy of the Library
of Congress)

Italian mother
and baby in
Lower East Side
tenement. (Photo
by Jacob A. Riis—
Courtesy of the
Museum of the
City of New York)

Italian immigrant
family sharing
their one room
apartment in a
Lower East Side
tenement. (Photo
by Jesse Tarbox
Beals—Courtesy
of the Museum
of the City of
New York)

Left: Pietro learning to write. (Photo by Jacob A. Riis—Courtesy of the Library of Congress)

Below: Members of Mutual Benefit Societies of Chicago in front of St. Philip Benizi Church. (Courtesy of the Italians in Chicago Project funded by an NEH grant)

Clockwise:

Bandit's Roost at 39 1/2 Mulberry Street about 1888.
(Photo by Jacob A. Riis—Courtesy of the Museum
of the City of New York)

Baxter Street—Rag Picker's Row. (Photo by Jacob A.
Riis—Courtesy of the Museum of the City of New York)

Children of Italian immigrants who lived in tenements
of South Philadelphia around 1900. These buildings
were stifling in summer, freezing in winter and rat-
infested. (Courtesy of the Urban Archives Center of Temple University)

An Italian family trying to make a home in the basement
of a cramped South Philadelphia tenement around 1900.
(Courtesy of the Urban Archives Center of Temple University)

ical, and educational assistance to their immigrant members. Some of these societies even helped found settlement houses that conducted programs specifically designed to introduce immigrants to American laws, ways, and traditions. By 1920 there were more than 2,500 Italian mutual-aid societies and fraternal organizations located throughout the country. Membership numbered in the hundreds of thousands. Eventually, many of these organizations would gradually evolve into social clubs sponsoring festivals, dinners, dances, picnics, and other recreational activities. For the Italian immigrant in the age of mass migration, however, they offered security, hope, and a sense of well-being.

Generoso Pope, whose leadership and ingenuity made *Il Progresso Italo-Americano*, the largest and most influential Italian Newspaper in the United States with a national circulation of 125,000 by 1922. (Courtesy of *Il Progresso Italo-Americano*)

Another institution that helped ease the transformation of the immigrant generation to American society was the Italian-language press. Daily and weekly newspapers, written almost exclusively in Italian, kept the immigrants informed of the news events in Italy. They also published items of Italian-American community interest such as births, deaths, and marriages, as well as social, cultural, and recreational events. They offered advice to immigrants on solving their social and economic problems in

Italian Daily newspapers. (From *Gli Italiani Negli Stati Uniti l'America*, 1906)

the unfamiliar American environment. They discussed politics and presented a wide spectrum of political opinion. They gave the immigrant a sense of ethnic pride by publishing articles on the glories of the Roman Empire, the Renaissance, and other great events of Italy's past.

L'Eco d'Italia, the first Italian-language newspaper published in the United States, was

founded by Secchi de Casali in New York City in 1849. Although limited in circulation, the weekly newspaper made its mark as the voice of the Italian community of New York for nearly three decades. The first Italian-language daily, *Il Progresso Italo-Americano* was founded in New York in 1879 by Carlo Barsotti. Under the ownership of Generoso Pope, it became the largest and most influential Italian newspaper in the country with a national circulation of more than 125,000 by 1922. Chicago's oldest Italian-language newspaper *L'Italia* also gained a large national circulation, while Philadelphia's *L'Opinione* and Cleveland's *La Voce del Popolo Italiano* had wide circu-

The *Italian Tribune* building of Newark, New Jersey. (Courtesy of the Ethnic Studies Collection, University of Scranton)

lation throughout the Middle Atlantic States and Midwest. The foremost Italian newspaper on the west coast was San Francisco's *L'Eco della Patria*. By 1922 there were 190 Italian weeklies and dailies published throughout the United States. Even a number of English-language American newspapers, cognizant of the large and growing Italian immigrant population, published an Italian news column.

Religious institutions also figured prominently in the life of the Italian immigrant community in America. Although the overwhelming majority of Italian immigrants were Roman Catholic, they were slow to embrace the Roman Catholic Church in America. They found it dominated by the Irish, who initially showed little understanding of traditional Italian religious practices. For Italian's, religion was an amalgam of church doc-

trines, personal beliefs, superstitions, witchcraft, festivals, feasts, and processions, particularly for the *contadini* of the South. In Italy, women and children usually went to church services, while men seldom did. The Irish-American Catholic hierarchy found these Italian religious practices repugnant. For their part, Italians did not comprehend the stolid, remote, impersonal religious attitudes of the Irish-American Catholics. These circumstances caused some Italian immigrants to drift away from the Catholic Church. The situation also encouraged the major

Bishop Giovanni Battista Scalabrini, the "Father of the Immigrants." (Courtesy of the Center for Migration Studies)

Protestant sects in America to seek a large number of conversions among those Italian immigrants disillusioned with the Catholic Church in America. Protestants engaged several hundred ministers, teachers, and social workers in this conversion effort. They also financed more than three hundred churches in Italian communities; published numerous religious books, magazines, and pamphlets in Italian; and sponsored educational and recreational programs for the children of immigrants. Although their evangelical

Lifting a child up to kiss the statue of St. Joseph of Bagheria during a *festa* in Chicago. (Courtesy of the Italians in Chicago Project funded by an NEH grant)

The so-called "Race of the Saints" held annually in Jessup, Pennsylvania in honor of St. Ubaldo, who saved the Italian village of Gubbio from invasion in the twelfth century. Although this photo was taken in the late 1940s, the celebration and race continues to be held in Jessup. (Courtesy of John Povanda)

work gained some converts, the vast majority of Italians remained, at least nominally, within the Catholic fold.

Meanwhile, the hierarchy of the Roman Catholic Church in both Italy and America met in council to devise ways of meeting the spiritual needs of the Italian-

Festa of St. Rocco in New York City. (Courtesy of the New York Public Library)

Americans. The Church enlisted religious orders to establish missions, churches, schools, and social centers in the Italian immigrant communities. Though Franciscans, Jesuits, Pallotines, and Salesians participated in this effort, the Scalabrinians, founded by Bishop Giovanni Battista Scalabrini, seemed to have the greatest impact on the Italian-Americans. Scalabrini, also known as the "Father of the Immigrants," founded the Apostolic College of Priests in Italy, a seminary that trained Italian priests for missionary work in Italian-American neighborhoods. The Scalabrinians

opened dozens of missions and encouraged the establishment of national parishes, schools, and social centers in Italian immigrant communities throughout America. They helped organize the celebration of the *festa* (an ancient festival in honor of the patron saint of each particular

Italian province or village). These festivals, celebrated in the "Little Italies" of America, entailed processions, music, street dancing, eating, drinking, and fire- works. The *festa* of Our Lady of Mount Carmel, Saint Rocco, and San Gennaro, which are still celebrated in the Italian-American neighborhoods of New York City today, attract several hundred-thousand people each year. The Scalabrinians used the financial proceeds from these kinds of events to support churches and parochial schools in the Italian immigrant communities. In such fashion they and other religious orders helped to bridge the gap between Italian immigrants and the Catholic Church in America.

Undoubtedly, the most significant religious figure sent by the Church to America to work among the Italian immigrants was Mother Francesca Xavier Cabrini. Born in Lombardy, Italy, in 1850, she founded the Missionary Sisters of the Sacred Heart in 1880 with the intention of laboring in China. Instead, ordered by Pope Leo XIII, she went to America in 1889 to work among the Italian immigrants. She and her Missionary Sisters ran schools, orphanages, nurseries, hospitals,

Women leading procession with banner of patron saint during *festa* of Our Lady of Mount Carmel. (Courtesy of Padre Terzo Vinci, Pastor of Our Lady of Mount Carmel Church)

St. Francis Xavier Cabrini. (Courtesy of Cabrini College)

and religious instruction for Italians throughout the United States. They worked in the tenement districts of New York, the mining towns of Colorado and Minnesota, the lumber camps of Washington and Oregon, and the disease-ridden slums of New Orleans. For this work she recruited more than 4,000 sisters. In 1909 she became a citizen of the United States, but eventually she continued her missionary efforts for the Italian immigrant communities of Central and South America. Shortly after her death in 1917, her followers promoted her for sainthood. She was beatified on November 13, 1938 and canonized on July 7, 1946, the first American citizen raised to sainthood.

Rev. Pietro Bandini, the founder of Tontitown, Arkansas. (Courtesy of Washington Historical Society in Fayetteville, Arkansas)

Not all of the Italian immigrants who came to the United States in the period of the great migration settled in the middle Atlantic states or in one of the Little Italies of urban America. A considerable minority settled in the South, Southwest, and West. In the South and Southwest, Italians formed farm colonies and raised cotton, grapes, sugar cane, and tobacco. Although most of these agricultural colonies did not profit greatly, a few of them succeeded, such as those in Bryan in Texas, Verdella in Missouri, and Tontitown in Arkansas. The latter, founded by Father Pietro Bandini, a Scalabrinian priest from Italy, was one of the most successful farm communities. Father Bandini purchased a tract of land in the Ozarks of Arkansas for a dollar an acre from the St. Louis and San Francisco Railroad; and in 1898 he led forty Italian immigrant families to the land. They named their settlement Tontitown, after the Italian explorer Enrico Di Tonti, who two centuries earlier had been one of the first men to explore the Arkansas Territory. Despite initial difficulties with native-born Americans, weather, and climate, Tontitown became a successful agricultural community, producing grapes, vegetables, and dairy products. In the West, Italian farm settlements sprang up in Colorado, Washington, Oregon, and

Charles A. Siringo.
(Courtesy of
University of Texas
Library at Austin)

California. The largest and most successful of these settlements developed in California, the soil and climate of which was well suited for growing every sort of farm crop. Grape growing proved particularly lucrative. Besides farming, Italians were attracted to the mining, fishing, and wine-making industries in California. The lands west of the Mississippi even bred a few unconventional venturesome types such as the Italian-American cowboy, Charles Angelo Siringo. He is reported to be the first cowboy to publish an autobiography. Entitled *A Texas Cowboy*, it sold more than one million copies. His other books also met with considerable success. Most Italian immigrants in the American West, however, worked in more conventional occupations.

41

CHAPTER THREE

FEAR, PREJUDICE, AND DISCRIMINATION

The mass migration of Italians to America in the last decades of the nineteenth and early decades of the twentieth centuries helped spur a resurgence of "nativism" in the United States. Coming principally from the southern provinces of Italy, these "new immigrants" were culturally far different from both native-born Americans and their compatriots who had earlier come from northern Italy. To America, the *contadini* from southern Italy were poor, illiterate, and politically backward. They tended to settle in the clannish environments of Little Italies located in the big cities along the Atlantic seaboard. To native-born Americans it appeared that they were incapable of becoming good American citizens because so many of them were transient. Thousands of them were single men between the ages of sixteen and forty-five who arrived in America each year to work, with the sole purpose of earning enough money to return home to Italy to establish a higher-quality life. Many native-born Americans viewed these Italians as "birds of passage," who seemed interested only in taking the wealth of America without contributing anything in return. The fact that the vast majority of native-born Americans were Protestant caused even greater mistrust. Furthermore, these Italian immigrants came at a time of profound economic upheaval in America. The frontier had closed, and Americans sincerely doubted whether the unlimited flow of immigrants could be continually absorbed into the economy.

These concerns led native-born Americans to begin to demand federal legislation to restrict immigration. In 1882 Congress passed legislation restricting paupers, convicts, lunatics, and idiots from immigrating to the United States. In 1891 Congress passed legislation that forbade American employers from recruiting laborers in foreign countries, and denied admission to those with contagious diseases. Strong sentiment for the passage of a "literacy test" for admission existed in the 1890s. The Immigration

Restriction League, a newly formed New England nativist organization, persistently supported the literacy test bill, which passed both houses of Congress in 1897. President Cleveland, however, vetoed it. This proposal would have excessively restricted emigration from eastern and southern Europe, particularly the migration of the *contadini* from southern Italy, had it become law. In 1887 the American Protective Association came into existence. This anti-alien and anti-Catholic organization enlisted the support of native-born American laborers throughout the country, and waged a bitter campaign against Italian and other immigrant workers. The association claimed that the low expectations of immigrant laborers undermined the wages and job security of American labor. The fact that the American Protective Association and the Immigrant Restriction League gained such wide support reflected the growing concern of native-born Americans that if unrestricted immigration continued, the very foundation of American society would be endangered.

Mob attacking Italians in the prison courtyard in New Orleans. (From *Harper's Weekly*, 1891)

American nativists actually had little knowledge of the culture and lifestyle of Italian immigrants and often stereotyped them as dumb, dirty, dishonest, violent, and semibarbarous slum dwellers. One restrictionist spokesman, Senator Henry Cabot Lodge of Massachusetts, suggested that the entry gates to America should not be left "unguarded" to the undesirable southern Italian immigrant. A significant segment of the American press echoed similar sentiments. Racists began to use slurs such as "dago," "wop," and "guinea" when referring to Italians. In certain southern states, Italians were segregated in schools and other public institutions just as African-Americans were. Many native-born Americans came to believe that all Italians were somehow connected with sinister criminal organizations such as the "Black Hand" and "Mafia," even though the vast majority of Italians were peaceful, law-abiding people.

Prejudice against Italians at times resulted in violence. One such incident occurred in New Orleans in 1891. While investigating the criminal activities of two rival Sicilian gangs, David C. Hennessy, the chief of police of the city, was mortally wounded. Before he died, however, he said that five Italians had ambushed and

New Orleans Police Chief David Hennessy reputedly murdered by the Italian "Mafia" of New Orleans. (Courtesy of the Tulane University Library)

shot him. Even though Hennessy could not identify his murderers, Mayor Joseph A. Shakespeare was convinced that the Mafia had committed the murder. The police were ordered into Italian neighborhoods and told to arrest all possible suspects. More than one hundred Italians were arrested, but only nineteen were accused of the crime and bound over for trial. Ten were to be tried for plotting Hennessy's murder and nine for actually committing the murder. During the trial of the nine, the jury found six of the defendants not guilty, and the judge declared mistrials in the cases of the other three. Incensed by the verdict, a number of the leading citizens of New Orleans formed a "vigilance committee," stormed the jail, and murdered the ten Italian prisoners who

were still awaiting trial. For good measure they publicly lynched another Italian who was serving a minor sentence for some petty crime. This incident so outraged the Italian government in Rome that it recalled its ministers and broke all

In the gallery of the prison where three Italian prisoners were shot and clubbed to death. (Courtesy of *Illustrated American*, 1891)

45

diplomatic relations with the United States until a substantial financial payment of restitution was made to the families of the victims. Anti-Italian sentiment also resulted in several other violent incidents, including lynchings of Italians in Colorado, Louisiana, and Mississippi during the 1890s. This violence continued well into the twentieth century.

Two Italians managed to save their lives by hiding in the prison dog house. (Courtesy of the *Illustrated American*, 1891)

No historical incident demonstrates the prejudice against Italians more than the Sacco-Vanzetti case. On April 15, 1920, the paymaster and a guard of the Slater and Morrill Shoe Factory in Massachusetts were murdered on a street in South Braintree. The payroll of $16,000 was seized by unidentified men who drove away in a speeding automobile. A few weeks later Nicolo Sacco, a shoemaker, and Bartolomeo Vanzetti, a fish peddler, were arrested and indicted for the crime. Both men were Italian immigrants and also anarchists. They had encouraged strikes and organized protest meetings against the infamous Palmer Raids of 1919 and 1920. The trial of Sacco and Vanzetti, which began on May 31, 1921, became one of the great travesties of the American system of justice. The presiding judge, Webster Thayer, had privately referred to Sacco and Vanzetti as "those anarchist bastards." Purely circumstantial evidence, witnesses of questionable reliability, and a prejudiced judge convinced a jury of native-

The coroner holding a brief inquest on the bodies which had been brought into two narrow cells in the prison. (Courtesy of the *Illustrated American*, 1891)

Left: Nicola Sacco, a shoe factory employee, shortly after his arrest for the robbery and murder of two employees of the Slater and Morrill Shoe Factory in Braintree, Massachusetts. (Courtesy of the Boston Public Library)

Right: Bartolomeo Vanzetti, a fish peddler, who was convicted with Nicola Sacco for the Braintree murder and robbery in 1919. (Courtesy of the Boston Public Library)

born Americans that the defendants were guilty. On July 14, 1921, Sacco and Vanzetti received a death sentence. Their execution, however, was postponed for nearly six years.

The case had become the cause célèbre of the 1920s. Throughout the United States and even in Europe radical supporters of labor and liberal sympathizers demanded the release of the two men. "Save Sacco and Vanzetti" became a slogan heard throughout the United States and Italy. Major demonstrations of protest took place in front of the American Embassy in Rome. Italian-Americans established the Sacco-Vanzetti Defense Committee, which raised substantial funds to pay the legal costs incurred by the series of appeals to

Nicola Sacco (center left) and Bartolomeo Vanzetti (center right) guarded by deputy sheriffs as they leave the Norfolk County Courthouse in Massachusetts. (Courtesy of the Library of Congress)

gain a new trial. In response to public pressure, Massachusetts Governor Alvin T. Faller formed a special commission of prominent American citizens to review the case. Although the report of the commission indicated some of the evidence was flimsy, it ruled that there had been no prejudice in the trial of the two Italians. When Sacco and Vanzetti appeared before the court to be sentenced to death by Judge Thayer, Vanzetti told the court: "I am suffering because I am a radical, and indeed I am a radical; I have suffered because I was an Italian, and indeed I am an Italian." Sacco and Vanzetti were electrocuted on August 23, 1927.

Judge Webster Thayer, who presided over the trial of Sacco and Vanzetti, privately referred to them as "Dagos" and "Sons of Bitches." (Courtesy of the Boston Public Library)

Another manifestation of nativism and xenophobia in the early twenties was the resurrection of the Ku Klux Klan by William Simmons, an evangelist and ex-army officer in Georgia in 1915. Although it bore certain resemblances to the former Ku Klux Klan, the new Klan was inspired by an exaggerated nationalism and a growing intolerance toward radicalism and nonconformism that had emerged in America during the period of World War I. The Klan remained primarily a Georgia, organization until 1920, when Simmons engaged the public relations services of Edward Clark and Elizabeth Tyler who publicized the Klan throughout the nation. By 1924, nearly five million Americans had become members. The Klan extended to such non-Southern states as Indiana, Oregon, and

A Ku Klux Klan meeting in Chicago in the 1920s which attracted more than 30,000 members of the Klan. (Courtesy of the Library of Congress)

California. Comprised of Protestant and native-born Americans, it attacked Italian-Americans as recent immigrants, radicals, and Roman Catholics. Although its membership declined significantly after 1925, the animosity that the Klan and other nativist organizations had generated toward aliens in America had resulted in a series of restrictive laws that changed the entire American immigration system. The Quota Act of 1921 and the Johnson Reed Act of 1924 turned the flood of eastern and southern European immigration across the Atlantic to a trickle. The Great Depression, which began in 1929, further reinforced America's restrictive immigration policies. With more than fourteen million unemployed workers in the 1930s, it was very unlikely that America would reopen its borders to aliens.

Benito Mussolini speaking to a massive crowd in Italy during the 1930s. (Courtesy of the Library of Congress)

Most Italian-Americans struggled along with the rest of the population during the hard economic times of the Depression. A few, however, returned to Italy. Perhaps they were enthralled with Benito Mussolini and Fascism. Mussolini had created the impression that he had put Italy on the road to political and economic stability. He boasted continually of Italian heritage, patriotism, and greatness. At first, most Italian-Americans admired Mussolini for the prestige and respect he had gained for Italy in the world community. A substantial element of the Italian-language press, including the popular *Il Progresso Italo-Americano*, supported the efforts of *Il Duce*. He sent agents to the United States and spent huge sums of money to proselytize Italian-Americans with the doctrines of Fascism. As early as 1925, the Fascist League of North America came into existence. Claiming a membership of more than 12,000 Italian-Americans, the League coordinated Fascist activities and propaganda throughout America. Italian-Americans applauded *Il Duce* when he concluded the Lateran Treaty with the Catholic Church in Rome in 1929. This agreement ended the long-standing hostility between the Italian state and the Church. Its provisions established the sovereign state of the Vatican City within Rome, restored the temporal power of the pope, and sanctioned the right of the Church to operate schools and other institutions in Italy. In turn, the Church recognized the Italian government in Rome as legitimate.

Left: Arturo Toscanini, world famous symphony leader who left Italy having become disillusioned with the Fascist Regime of Benito Mussolini. (Courtesy of the New York Public Library at Lincoln Center)

Right: Enrico Fermi, a winner of the Nobel Prize in Physics who fled Italy during Mussolini's tenure in office. (Photo by H.M. Agnew—Courtesy of General Atomic Company)

When Mussolini's unscrupulous politics and curtailment of individual liberties became known, support among Italian-Americans for his regime began to decline. Italian anti-Fascist exiles such as Max Ascoli, Gaetano Salvemini, Arturo Toscanini, Enrico Fermi, and others revealed the less glorious and more oppressive aspects of Fascism. These prominent refugees helped establish anti-Fascist organizations in America, including the Friends of Italian Freedom and the Mazzini Society. They published articles, books, and pamphlets that condemned the doctrines of Fascism and the criminal practices of Mussolini's regime. Carlo Tresca, an Italian-American socialist and journalist, and Luigi Antonini, the president of the International Ladies Garment Workers Union, opposed Fascism because they believed that it undermined the rising power of the working class in both Italy and America.

Not until Italy attacked Ethiopia and joined in an alliance with Hitler's Germany did Musso-

President Franklin Delano Roosevelt seemed to exhibit some disdain for Italians when he remarked that "the hand that held the dagger has struck it into the back of its neighbor," when he referred to Italy joining Germany in the invasion of France. (Courtesy of the Library of Congress)

lini lose the enthusiastic support he had enjoyed from so many Italian-Americans. Simultaneously, prejudice against Italian-Americans became more acute in the anti-Fascist atmosphere in the United States during the late 1930s. When Italy joined Germany in the invasion of France in 1940, Italians in America began to feel the full brunt of this discrimination. Even President Franklin Roosevelt showed a degree of dis-

Carlo Tresca, anti-fascist editor and labor leader. (Courtesy of the Archives of Labor and Urban Affairs, Wayne State University)

dain for the Italian-American community when he remarked that "the hand that held the dagger has struck it into the back of its neighbor." American newspapers, magazines, and radio broadcasts began to question the loyalty of Italian-Americans to the United States. Shortly after the attack on Pearl Harbor, the more than 600,000 Italians in America who were not yet citizens were forced to register as enemy aliens. A few politicians suggested that these aliens forfeit their property and businesses, while

Luigi Antonini, President of the International Ladies' Garment Workers Union, who opposed bitterly Mussolini's fascism. (Courtesy of the ILGWU Archives)

others proposed confining them in detention camps. Fortunately, these plans were abandoned in 1942 when it had been discovered that only 228 of the more than 600,000 Italian aliens could be properly classified as "enemies." The fact that over 500,000 Italian-Americans served in the armed forces of the United States during World War II helped remove the stigma of "enemy" from the Italians in America.

The association of criminality, nevertheless, has stuck with Italians in America for nearly an entire century. Even today some Americans seem to have the impression that all Italians or Americans of Italian descent are involved with secret conspiratorial criminal organizations such as the Mafia, Black Hand, and *Cosa Nostra*. Over the years, the American press and media have contributed to typecasting Italian-Americans as members of these sinister organizations. However, like most stereotypes, the perception of Italian-Americans as "Mafia" owes its origin to a certain degree of historical fact.

Historically, the term "Mafia" signified a form of criminality that arose in western Sicily during the eighteenth century as a result of the deep distrust of the Sicilian government and its ability to administer justice. This situation resulted in the practice of individuals settling disputes privately and punishing crimes and other wrongs by direct personal action. When the government of Sicily collapsed during the period of the Napoleonic invasions, justice came to be administered entirely by shrewd, cunning, opportunistic, and often unscrupulous individuals who came to be referred to as *mafiosi*. Between 1820 and 1848 the Mafia, as groups of *mafiosi* were called, became firmly established in Sicilian society when the old aristocracy of Sicily employed them to suppress the peasant uprisings of the period. The Mafia gradually obtained such power that they became a type of unofficial government for Sicily.

The members of the Mafia followed a complicated code of traditions known as the *omertà*, which entailed absolute silence about the activities of members, the obligation never to seek justice from legally constituted authorities, a responsibility to come to the aid of a fellow member in trouble, and reserving the right to avenge injuries to members and their families. Mafia activities included robbery, blackmail, extortion, and murder. All proceeds from Mafia activities were supposed to go to the group as a whole. After the unification of Italy in 1860 the new Italian government attempted to suppress the Mafia. Government efforts were impeded by corrupt politicians who protected the Mafia in order to gain its assistance in controlling elections. In the 1920s Mussolini launched an intensive campaign against the Mafia, and he nearly succeeded in destroying it. The Mafia, however, reemerged during World War II.

The Mafia came to America during the mass migration of southern Italians, which began in the 1880s. The early Mafia in America found considerable opportunities in the Little Italies of New York, Philadelphia, Chicago, and New Orleans. Unlike the Mafia in Sicily, however, the Mafia in America operated more on an individual and independent basis. The American Mafia used the ancient symbol of the Black Hand to

The remains of Police Lieutenant Joseph Petrosino arriving at his widow's home in 1909. (Courtesy of the Library of Congress)

**Albert Anastasia.
(Courtesy of the
U.S. Department
of Justice)**

threaten newly arriving Italian immigrants into acceding to their demands. Extortion, kidnapping, thefts, and assaults ranked among the principal crimes committed by these Black Hand terrorists. The chief victims were usually peddlers, shopkeepers, truck farmers, and laborers. Occasionally, the early Mafia resorted to murder. The killing of Police Chief David C. Hennessy of New Orleans in 1891 brought the Mafia into prominence in America. In Chicago, the Black Hand so victimized Italian-Americans that the community formed the White Hand Society in 1907 in an effort to bring law and order to the city. New York City formed the Italian Squad through the police department, headed by Lieutenant Joseph Petrosino, in an effort to curb Mafia Black Hand activities in the city. Petrosino even went so far as to journey to Sicily in an attempt to uncover links between the Sicilian and New York Mafias. Shortly after his arrival in Palermo in 1909, he was shot to death by two unknown assailants. His work against organized crime in New York, however, was later carried on by other Italian-Americans such as Mario Biaggi and Ralph Salerno. Biaggi's efforts against organized crime made him the most decorated police officer in the history of New York City.

It was not until the 1920s that the Mafia moved from intra-community crime, practiced in the Italian ethnic neighborhoods, to organized crime on a national scale. The passage of the Volstead Act of 1920, which prohibited the sale and consumption of alcoholic beverages, opened the door to a new wave of organized crime in the United States. Italian gangs soon found themselves fighting with Irish, Jewish, and German gangs for control of the lucrative bootlegging operations in New York, Chicago, Boston, and Detroit. By 1930 the Italian Mafia dominated not only the illegal liquor industry, but they also had extended their operations to gambling, prostitution, loan-sharking, narcotics trafficking, labor, and industrial racketeering. They garnered millions of dollars in profits from their national crime syndicates. Some of the most prominent Italian gangsters of this era were Alphonse Capone, Jim Colosimo, John Torrio, Guiseppe Masseria, Salvatore Maranzano, and Frank Costello. Through the thirties and forties such notables as Salvatore "Lucky" Luciano, Joseph Lanza, Joe Adonis, Albert Anastasia, Frank Lanzia, Vito Genovese, Joseph Bonnano, Carlo Gambino, Joseph Profaci, and Joseph Columbo emerged as major organized crime figures.

By far the paradigm of the Italian gangster in America in the 1920s was Alphonse Capone. Born in Naples in 1899, Capone was brought by his parents to America as a child. He grew up in the slums of Brooklyn, New York, and left school after the fourth grade. As a youngster, he earned a living by extorting money from Italian grocers and fruit stand operators in Brooklyn. Brought to Chicago in 1920 by mobster John Torrio, Capone soon became the czar of crime in that city. He was also referred to as the unofficial mayor of Chicago, because he had so many police and public officials on his payroll. A friend of the rich and famous in Chicago society, Capone once boasted, "All I do is supply a public demand. I do it in the best way and least harmful way I can." It was Al Capone who undoubtedly engineered the St. Valentine's Day Massacre in 1929 in which seven rival gang members were brutally murdered in a garage. The Internal Revenue Service eventually caught up with

Salvatore "Lucky" Luciano. (Courtesy of the U.S. Department of Justice)

Capone, and indicted him on charges of tax evasion in 1931. Convicted of these charges, he went to prison, where he spent most of his life until his death in 1947.

Overwhelming evidence supports the fact that in the last century Italian-Americans have been a dominant force in organized crime in the United States. The Mafia, however, was never the all powerful multifarious national syndicate that certain elements of the American press and media have suggested. Futhermore, it is estimated

Rogue's Gallery
portrait of Al Capone.
(Courtesy of the
Chicago Historical
Society)

Below: The St.
Valentine's Day
Massacre of 1929
which has been attrib-
uted to Al Capone.
(Courtesy of the
Chicago Historical
Society)

today there are less than a dozen Mafia crime families with a membership of a few hundred—scattered in major cities—throughout the United States. With the Italian-American population in the United States numbering between ten and fifteen million, it is safe to conclude that more than ninety-nine percent of Italian-Americans have no affiliation with the Mafia. Unfortunately, notorious Italian criminals such as Capone, Costello, and Luciano have tarnished the reputation of the honest and law-abiding millions of Italians in America.

Charles J. Bonaparte who founded the FBI in 1905. (Courtesy of the Library of Congress)

On the right side of the law, many thousands of Italian-American police officers, prosecutors, and other law enforcement officials were bringing the justice system to the criminals. In 1908 President Theodore Roosevelt appointed the Baltimore-born, Harvard-educated lawyer Charles J. Bonaparte as U. S. Attorney General. It was Bonaparte who issued the order that created a special investigative force as a permanent subdivision of the Department of Justice, a special force that was later renamed the Federal Bureau of Investigation.

In 1993 President William J. Clinton appointed Louis J. Freeh, son of Bernice Chianciola, to be Director of

Louis J. Freeh served as Director of the FBI from 1993 to 2001. (Courtesy of Louis J. Freeh)

the FBI. Freeh had served as an FBI Special Agent from 1975 to 1981 in the New York City field office and at FBI headquarters in Washington, D.C. In 1981 he joined the U. S. Attorney's Office for the Southern District of New York. While in New York, he headed the Organized Crime Unit, and became the leading prosecutor in the "Pizza Connection" case, which involved extensive drug trafficking by Sicilian organized crime members using pizza parlors as covers. Freeh's successful prosecution of the long and complex case resulted in the government convicting sixteen of the seventeen codefendants.

Rudolph W. Guiliani, later Mayor of New York, also became U. S. Attorney for the Southern District of New York in 1983. He led the effort to jail drug dealers, fought organized crime, and broke the labyrinth of corruption in government. He also prosecuted numerous high-profile white-collar criminal cases including those of Michael Milken and Ivan Boesky. Still another Italian-American New York District Attorney, Diane Giacalone, continually prosecuted John Gotti until his conviction in 1992.

CHAPTER FOUR

ECONOMIC AND POLITICAL ACCOMPLISHMENTS

Although most Italian immigrants who arrived in the United States after 1880 came from rural agricultural backgrounds, few of them settled in the farming regions of America. Practical economic necessity explains this phenomenon. First, the best agricultural lands in the country had already been settled by 1880. Second, most immigrants on their arrival to America only had enough money to last a few days, much less to travel to agricultural areas. Third, few could speak or understand the English language, further restricting their mobility. Fourth, many had been disillusioned with the harsh struggle for survival in the *Mezzogiorno* and wanted a new way of life in America. Fifth, some had no intention of settling permanently in America, which farm life would tend to assure. Finally, and most importantly, American industry needed immigrant laborers. Therefore, the poor, illiterate, and unskilled Italian immigrant settled in the large industrial areas of America where jobs were available.

Italian immigrants often entered the American labor force through the *padrone* system. The *padrone* (or boss) was usually a shrewd Italian who had come to America a few years earlier and who spoke enough English to serve as an interpreter for the newly arrived immigrant. The *padrone* had contacts with American employers that were instrumental in getting work for immigrants. For his services he charged

The *Padrone.*
(Steiner, *On the Trail of the Immigrant,* 1906)

59

Padrones on White Bog in Browns Hills, New Jersey. Chief padrone in straw hat is Gus Donato. (Courtesy of the Library of Congress)

the employer and the worker a fee. He often ran a boarding home which provided the worker with room, board, and miscellaneous services. At times he overcharged for food. Some unscrupulous *padroni*, in collusion with employers, took advantage of the immigrants by binding them to long work periods at very low wages. Not all *padroni* were evil, however. Certain *padroni* helped the immigrants learn English and gain American citizenship. They assisted immigrants in obtaining better housing. If the immigrant got into trouble with the law, the *padroni* gave legal advice. Others provided banking, real estate, and letter writing services.

Despite the many hardships they had to endure, often at the hands of dishonest *padroni*, the Italian immigrants gave full measure of their labor. They took whatever jobs were offered to them and usually worked under the most unhealthful and dangerous conditions. They wielded the pick and the shovel, mixed cement, and carried bricks on construction jobs. They built roads, bridges, tunnels, canals, subways, and skyscrapers. They mined anthracite coal in Pennsylvania and bituminous coal in West Virginia, Kentucky, and Illinois. They labored in the silver and copper mines of Arizona and Colorado, and in the iron mines of Michigan and Minnesota. In Chicago and Kansas City they manned the stockyards and slaughterhouses. They made cigars

Italian workers canning asparagus in California plant about 1890. (Courtesy of Del Monte Corporation)

Below: Italian immigrants living in boxcars while working on the railroad in Butte, Montana about 1904. (Courtesy of the Italians in Chicago Project funded by an NEH grant)

in Florida and manufactured textiles and clothing in the sweatshops of New York, New Jersey, and the New England states. Thousands of Italian women and children were employed in the textile and garment industries. Some families even took piecework home for extra pay.

The average weekly salary of the Italian male immigrant in 1900 ranged between ten dollars and fifteen dollars per week. Because employment of unskilled labor was not always in demand, the average Italian male earned less than $600 per year. The average native-born American earned more than $1,200 per year. It is not surprising, therefore, that employers sought to use Italian immigrants as strikebreakers and scabs to threaten the newly developing labor unions in America. Italian laborers became involved in unfortunate incidents with striking union coal miners in Pennsylvania, meatpackers in Chicago, and garment workers in New York. Although they often were

Group of Breaker Boys in #9 Breaker, Hughestown Borough, Pennsylvania Coal Company. Smallest boy is Angelo Ross. (Courtesy of the Library of Congress)

Italian track-walker on Pennsylvania Railroad near New York City. (Photo by Lewis W. Hine—Courtesy of the New York Public Library)

Below: A common sight in major cities at the turn of the century was the Italian bootblack. (Courtesy of the Library of Congress)

Two young Italian bootblacks in New York City pose for photographers. (Courtesy of the Library of Congress)

Immigrant mother and children making artificial flowers to help supplement the income of the father of the family, who as a day laborer, earned $1.50 per day. (Photo by Jessie Tarbox Beals—Courtesy of The Museum of the City of New York)

ignorant of the fact that they were being used as strikebreakers, Italians gained a bad reputation among union workers. Certain unions barred them from membership in the early years of unionization. Eventually Italians joined labor unions and demanded better wages and working conditions. They came to

IRT subway construction performed by Italian laborers about 1901. (Courtesy of New York Historical Society)

champion union causes and to lead some of the most celebrated strikes in the history of the American labor movement.

The famous textile workers' strike in Lawrence, Massachusetts, in 1912, was organized by Italian workers and labor leaders. Under the banner of the Industrial Workers of the World, Arturo Giovannitti led 15,000 Italian and non-Italian immigrants in a demonstration against the American Woolen Company. This strike called national attention to the horrid working conditions and the violations of child labor laws that

Lawrence, Massachusetts textile strikers, led by members of the IWW in 1912 are met by bayonets. (Courtesy of the Library of Congress)

Arturo Giovannitti (left) and IWW organizer Joseph Ettor photographed after they were arrested during the Lawrence, Massachusetts textile strike of 1912. (Courtesy of the Archives of Labor and Urban Affairs, Wayne State University)

were practiced by the garment industries in New England. The following year Carlo Tresca, another fiery Italian labor organizer, led immigrant workers in a dramatic but less-successful strike against several silk mills in Paterson, New Jersey. Meanwhile, Luigi Antonini organized the largest local chapter of the International Ladies Garment Workers Union, and August Bellanca headed the Italian workers of the Amalgamated Clothing Workers of America. George Baldanzi and James Petrillo became presidents of the Textile Workers of America and Musicians' Union respectively.

By the 1930s Italians had risen from pick and shovel work to more skilled jobs. They stopped laboring in the menial occupations of bootblacks, pushcart peddlers, and organ grinders to owning and managing more enterprising businesses such as shoe-shine parlors, grocery stores, fruit markets, butcher shops, bakeries, shoe repair shops,

Left: James C. Petrillo, long-time president of the American Federation of Musicians. (Courtesy of the American Federation of Musicians)

Right: Luigi Antonini, organizer of the largest local of the International Ladies' Garment Workers' Union. (Courtesy of the ILGWU archives)

Left: Interior of Antonio's and Angelina's grocery store at 40 E. 115 Street in the Roseland nieghborhood of Chicago. (Courtesy of Italians in Chicago Project funded by an NEH grant)

Below: Gonnella bakery wagons and employees on Sangamon Street in Chicago about 1900. (Courtesy of the Italians in Chicago Project funded by an NEH grant)

Right: Italian-American fruit stand on Broadway in New York City about 1935. (Courtesy of Joseph DeMichele)

Below: Italian woman bread peddler just off Mulberry Street in New York City. (Courtesy of the Library of Congress)

Above left: Italian shoemaker in Pennsylvania. (Courtesy of the Ethnic Studies Collection of the University of Scranton)

Above right: Original home of Paul Revere in Boston, later converted to an Italian bank and cigar store. (Courtesy of the Library of Congress)

Left: Italian bread store at 59 Bleeker Street in New York's "Little Italy." (Photo by Berenice Abbott—Courtesy of the Museum of the City of New York)

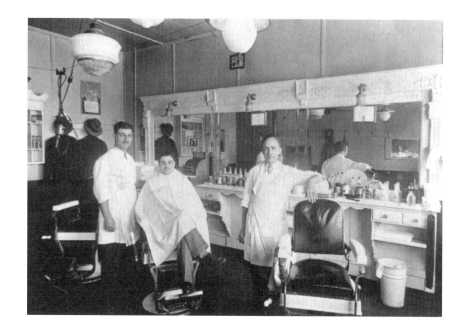

Italian barber shop in Scranton, Pennsylvania about 1930. (Courtesy of Pasquale Lentini)

barber shops, tailor shops, and confectioneries. They opened hotels, restaurants, and saloons. A few entered the food import-export business, and many entered the construction businesses. Others prospered as carpenters, plumbers, electricians, painters, masons, and machinists.

Italian immigrants who settled outside large urban centers met with considerable success in agricultural enterprises. Particularly profitable agricultural ventures were truck farms that supplied fruits and vegetables to American cities throughout the country. Three of the most famous of the dozens of successful farm communities founded by Italian immigrants are Vineland, New Jersey; Tontitown, Arkansas; and the Italian Swiss colony of California. The state of California with its excellent soil and climate, held special attraction for those Italian immigrants who entered agricultural occupations. As early as 1900, there were more than sixty thousand Italian immigrants cultivating orchards, farms, and vineyards in the Golden

Italian immigrant families harvesting black berries in Vineland, New Jersey. (Courtesy of the Vineland Historical and Antiquarian Society, New Jersey)

State. The productive vineyards soon established wine making as one of the largest and most profitable industries in the state.

Vineland Municipal Band in 1900 composed almost entirely of Italian immigrant musicians. (Courtesy of the Vineland Historical and Antiquarian Society, New Jersey)

It was also in California that Amadeo Pietro Giannini, the son of an immigrant from Genoa, founded the Bank of America—the largest bank in the United States. Giannini began as a banker for Italian immigrants in San Francisco's North Beach. When the San Francisco earthquake and fire struck in 1906, he wheeled from his bank more than two million dollars of his assets in a fruit peddler's cart, and quickly reopened for business. While the ashes were still warm, Giannini traveled about the devastated city loaning money to those in dire need. He prospered mightily, and became a major factor in California's economy. He soon discovered the potential of branch banking, and expanded from real estate to industrial financing. He also expanded his banking operations from California to the East Coast of the United States. When he retired in 1945, he had established himself as one of the most respected businessmen in America and a symbol of success for Italian-Americans. G.P. Morisini, Andrea Sbarboro, and Felix Argenti were three other Italians who established remarkable careers in the fields of banking and finance in America.

Domenico Ghirardelli, the patriarch and founder of the Ghirardelli Chocolate Company was born in Rapallo, Italy in 1817, the son and apprentice of a chocolatier. Sailing first to Uruguay and then to Peru, in 1838 he opened a confectionary store in Lima. Lured by the discovery of gold at Sutter's Mill, Ghirardelli sailed to California. He spent a few months

A.P. Giannini, founder of Bank of America. (Courtesy of the Bank of America Archives)

71

Left: Drawing of the building where A.P. Giannini opened his first bank in 1904. (Courtesy of the Bank of America Archives)

Right: World Headquarters Building of the Bank of America in San Francisco. (Courtesy of the Bank of America Archives)

prospecting for gold in the fields near Sonora and Jamestown. Giving up on his search for the motherload, he opened a grocery store in nearby Stockton. He moved to San Francisco in 1852 where he established the Ghirardelli Chocolate Company. At about 1865 he discovered, perhaps by accident, that by hanging chocolate in a warm room, the cocoa butter will drain off, leaving a residue that can be converted into ground chocolate. Known as the Broma process, it is still the most common technique in the production of chocolate. In 1894, while visiting his native Rapallo, Ghirardelli died. The business he started in 1852 now converts tons of cocoa beans into millions of pounds of cocoa cake, ground chocolate, and sweet chocolate every year.

Amadeo Obici arrived in America from Treviso, Italy in 1889. He was twelve

Dominico Ghiradelli, founder of the Ghiradelli Chocolate Company in San Francisco over 150 years ago. (Courtesy of the Ghiradelli Chocolate Company)

years old and had twelve cents in his pocket. For a few years he worked in his uncle's fruit market in Scranton, Pennsylvania. Then at seventeen, he opened his own fruit stand in the neighboring community of Wilkes-Barre. In addition to produce, he sold roasted peanuts. The peanut business became so successful that he began to package the peanuts and distribute them to other dealers. In 1906 he incorporated the Planter's Peanut Company. By 1930 he had four major peanut plants in the United States and Canada, more than two thousand employees, and authorized capital from its stockholders in excess of $15,000,000. The trademark of "Mr. Peanut" became the universal symbol of Planter's products, and Obici became the "peanut king" of the world, as well as one of the wealthiest Italians in America.

"Mr. Peanut." (Courtesy of Planters, A division of Nabisco Brands, Inc.)

Also in the food business, Giuseppe Taormiao, a Sicilian-born immigrant, parlayed his food-peddling business to Italian workers in New Orleans into the nationally known Progresso Company. Hector Boiardi began his career as an apprentice chef at the age of nine in his native Italy. After immigrating to America, he worked as a chef in New York City and Cleveland, Ohio, becoming famous for his spaghetti sauce. In 1929 Chef-Boy-Ar-Dee began to bottle his sauce for greater distribution and sales. Eventually he developed a complete line of processed Italian food products which are presently distributed throughout the country. In 1889 under the Del Monte label, an Italian immigrant named Marco Fontana founded the California Fruit Corporation, which became the largest fruit and vegetable canning company in the world. Two

Amadeo Obici, founder of the Planter Nut and Chocolate Company. (Courtesy of Joseph Rocereto)

73

Clockwise: Ernest and Julio Gallo. (Courtesy of E & J Gallo Winery)

Samuele Sebastiani, founder of Sebastiani Vineyards in California. (Courtesy of Sebastiani Vineyards)

Edmund A. Rossi, Jr., a founding member of the American Society of Enologists, currently directs winemaking and new products development for United Vintners, Inc. (Courtesy of United Vintners, Inc.)

Louis M. Martini, a founder of Louis M. Martini Winery. (Courtesy of Louis M. Martini Winery)

other Italians, Joseph and Rosario Di Giorgio founded the Di Giorgio Fruit Company which grew into the largest fresh produce shipping company in the world.

The success story of Jeno F. Paulucci, the son of an immigrant iron-ore miner, is legendary among American entrepreneurs. Shortly after World War II, Paulucci borrowed $2,500 to found the Chun King Corporation, which packaged Chinese food. In 1966 he sold Chun King to the R.J. Reynolds Tobacco Company for $63 million and founded Jeno's Inc., which became one of the world's leading packers of frozen pizza and snacks. In 1970 he came to head the Cornelius Company, a worldwide food and beverage dispensing corporation. He also served as the chairman of the National Italian-American Foundation and Chairman of the Board. Not only has he been honored numerous times, being cited as Italian-American of the Year on several occasions, but Jeno's Inc. has been honored as outstanding employer of the year from all the major corporations of the United States for its employment practices of hiring the handicapped.

Jeno F. Paulucci, founder of Jeno's Inc., and former National Chairman of the National Italian-American Foundation. (Courtesy of Jeno's Inc.)

Hector Boiardi, "Chef Boyardee." (Courtesy of American Home Foods)

Other notable Italian successes in the food industry include the La Rosa, Ronzoni, and Buitoni families, manufacturers of macaroni and pasta products; Nicholas D'Agostino, founder of the Buy Low grocery chain; Giuseppe Caccioppo, founder of the Grandview Dairy, Inc.; Pasquale Margarella, one of the largest manufacturers of Italian candy in America; and August Scolio, one of the largest fruit and produce wholesalers in New York. Dozens of Italians succeeded in the food import business by importing to America such foodstuffs as olives, olive oil, wine, cheese, vinegar, artichokes, tomatoes, tuna, sardines, and sausages. In California, Italians and

their descedants contributed substantially to the growth of the wine industry in America. Vintners such as Mondavi, Sebastiani, Petri, and Gallo made the California wine-making industry one of the biggest and most profitable businesses in the United States.

Thousands of Italian-Americans opened successful restaurants across the United States. These restauranteurs acquainted their patrons with spaghetti, ravioli, cannelloni, lasagna, prosciutto, salami, pepperoni, chicken cacciatore, veal parmigiana, scaloppini, minestrone, porchetto, saltimbocca, mussels, zucchini, zabaglione, spumone, and hundreds of other dishes. Pizza parlors have become a national institution in America. Although fine Italian restaurants can be found in nearly every metropolitan area of the United States, New York City boasts the largest number of dining establishments. Patsy's, founded by Pasquale "Patsy" Scognamillo, has been at the same location of 236 West 56th Street, in New York's theater district since it first opened in 1944. Offering the finest in Neapolitan Italian cuisine, Patsy's today attracts a varied clientele from loyal, regular patrons to tourists

Patsy's Italian Restaurant still at its' only location, 236 West 56th Street in New York City since 1944. (Courtesy of the Rubenstein Public Relations)

Ferrara's Bakery and Café, located at 195 Grand Street in New York's Little Italy is America's oldest pasticcieria in business since 1892. (Courtesy of Gabriella Lepore Gaspar)

and celebrities. Known for years as Frank Sinatra's favorite restaurant, Patsy's continues to be frequented by high-profile guests from both the East and West Coasts. Marchi's, located at 251 East 31st Street, opened with one small room in 1930, and has since grown considerably. At

Mary Ann Esposito, producer and host of the cooking show *Ciao Italia*, which has been airing on public television stations nationwide since 1989, and she is also the author of eight cookbooks. (Courtesy of Mary Ann Esposito)

Marchi's you are seated and served essentially the same kind of dinner offered patrons for nearly seventy-five years. At Marchi's you will feel like a guest for dinner in the home of a family that takes pride in its heritage. Forlini's at 93 Baxter Street and the

Robert Mondavi Winery in Oakville, California. (Courtesy of the Robert Mondavi Winery)

Left: Mario Batali, host of *Molto Mario, Mario Eats Italy* and *Ciao American* on the Food Network. (Courtesy of Mario Batali)

Right: Babbo Restorante e Enoteca, owned by Mario Batali and Joseph Bastianich in New York's Washington Square Park area, has won the James Best New Restaurant Award. (Courtesy of Mario Batali)

long-established Angelo's at 146 Mulberry Street are two of the best restaurants in Manhattan's Little Italy serving homemade pasta, a delectable selection of entrees, and hearty pastries and desserts. Sardi's at 234 West 44th Street, established in 1922, has been a rendezvous for politicians as well as celebrities of the theater, film, television, and sports for decades.

Babbo Ristorante e Enoteca opened by Mario Batali and Joseph Bastianich in 1998 at 110 Waverly Place in the center of New York's Greenwich Village has been a success from the day it opened, winning the James Beard Foundation's Best New Restaurant Award. Chef Batali's lusty creations incorporate the freshest seasonal produce, cheeses, meat, game, and seafood accented with fine Italian olive oils and many unusual ingredients, producing the best in Italian food. Since 1892 four generations of the Ferrara family have been delighting patrons at Ferrara's Bakery and Cafe at 195 Grand Street (between Mulberry and Molt Streets) with the finest in Italian desserts, such as cannoli, sfogliatella, and gelati along with expressos, lattés, and specialty coffees.

Philadelphia, with its sizeable Italian-American community, enjoys a large number

Alioto's, located at San Francisco's Fisherman's Wharf since 1925. It has been owned and operated by the Alioto family for three generations. (Courtesy of Alioto's)

of first-rate Italian restaurants. Ralph's at 760 South 9th Street in the heart of the Italian Market area has been in business since 1900 and is the oldest family-owned Italian restaurant in the country. Chef Jimmy Rubino, Jr., who is the fourth generation of his family to preside over Ralph's kitchen produces outstanding classic Italian food served in a family atmosphere. Everything is made-to-order with the finest ingredients from recipes that have been passed down from one generation to the next.

There are also numerous wonderful Italian-American restaurants on the West Coast, particularly in San Francisco, such as Alioto's. Located at San Francisco's Fisherman's Wharf since 1925, Alioto's has been owned and operated by the Alioto family for three generations and offers a stunning view of the Bay. Alioto's prepares fresh seafood and perfect Sicilian delicacies, seafood risotto, and shellfish cioppino. Fior d'Italia, 601 Union Street in North Beach's Union Square is another great Italian-American restaurant that opened in 1886, making it the oldest Italian restaurant in America. Today, under its third set of owners in 117 years, it offers the finest in traditional Italian cuisine and old-world service.

Ralph's, at 790 South Ninth Street in Philadelphia, has been in business since 1900 and is the oldest family owned Italian restaurant in the country. (Courtesy of Ralph's)

Italian-Americans have attained considerable prominence in America in the construction business. Clement Gaetano, Edward D. Agostini, Louis R. Perini, Robert Tosti, the Corbetta brothers, and the Paterno brothers were but a few of the major contractors who built roads, tunnels, bridges, apartment buildings, churches, libraries, and other public buildings throughout America. Generoso Pope, the editor of *Il Progresso Italo-Americano*, also founded the Colonial Sand and Stone Company, which became the largest construction material company in the world. Among the leaders of the printing industry, John F. Cuneo, headed of one of the largest printing firms in America.

In the 1970s and 1980s Italian-Americans began to rise to top executive positions in corporate America. Leading the way was Lee A. Iacocca, president of the Ford Motor Company, where he gave the world the Ford Mustang. As president of Chrysler Corporation, he is credited with saving the company from bankruptcy in the 1980s. And now, at the age of 80, he is running EV Motors, an electric cycle company, and has recently developed a spray-on version of Olivio, a butter substitute made from olive and canola oils.

At the age of thirty-nine, Ralph D. De Nunzio, the son of an immigrant father, was elected chairman of the New York Stock Exchange. Martin J. Casserio, vice president of General Motors, and Ross D. Siragusa, president of the Admiral Corporation helped pave the way for Italian-Americans to corporate leadership in America.

More recently, thousands of Italian-Americans have reached top executive positions in American corporations and businesses. Leonard Riggio is the founder and chairman of Barnes & Noble, Inc., the world's largest bookseller, which operates more

Left: Steve J. Belmonte is President and CEO of the Ramada Hotel chain and President and CEO of Hospitality Solutions. When he was only 18, he was the youngest General Manager in the history of the Holiday Inn chain. (Courtesy of Hospitality Solutions)

Right: John Paul DeJoria, son of immigrant parents from Italy and Greece, is the Co-Founder, President and CEO of Paul Mitchell Systems with sales exceeding $600,000,000 per year. (Courtesy of John Paul Mitchell Systems)

than three thousand retail stores and employs more than eighty thousand people. A visionary and brilliant marketer, he parlayed a single college bookstore into one of the largest and most successful retail enterprises in America. Another successful entrepreneur in the book business is Robert F. Di Romualdo, CEO and chairman of Borders, a chief·competitor of Barnes & Noble. Steven J. Belmonte was president and CEO of the Ramada Hotel chain for eleven years. In that time, he more than doubled the size of the chain and masterminded revolutionary customer initiatives. In 2002 he launched Hospitality Solutions, a nationwide consulting firm specializing in lodging industry issues at the hotel and corporative level. John Paul De Joria, son of immigrant parents from Italy and Greece, is the co-founder, president and CEO of Paul Mitchell Systems, which produces nearly one hundred different hairstyling products. The company generates sales exceeding $600,000,000 per year. One of the most powerful forces in the music industry is Tommy Mottola, the former CEO of Sony Music Entertainment. He is credited with launching the careers of such music superstars as Mariah Carey, Jennifer Lopez, and Celine Dion.

Patricia Fili-Krushel is executive vice president of administration at Time Warner, Inc., where she works closely with senior management on a variety of organizational, developmental, and diversity issues. She oversees corporate human resources, employee development and growth, compensation and benefits, and security. Prior to

Left: Patricia Russo is Chairperson and CEO of Lucent Technologies, one of the largest suppliers of communications hardware and services in the world. (Courtesy of Lucent Technologies)

Right: Patricia Fili-Krushel, Executive Vice-President of Administration for Time Warner, Inc. She was formerly CCA Web, M.D. Health and the first woman president of ABC Television. (Courtesy of Time Warner)

Above left: Nina DiSesa is Chairman and Chief Creative Officer of McCann-Erickson which is one of the top advertising agencies in the world. (Courtesy of McCann-Erickson Worldwide)

Above right: Music mogul Tommy Mottola celebrates award given to Academy Award winning actor Robert DeNiro at the National Italian-American Foundation Banquet. (Courtesy of NIAF)

joining Time Warner in July 2001, she was CEO of Web MD and from July 1998 to April 2000, she was president of ABC television network. In that capacity she moved ABC television network's ranking from third to first. Patricia Russo is chairman and CEO of Lucent Technologies, one of the largest suppliers of communications hardware, software, and services to the world's communications providers.

One of the top sports executives in the United States is Jerry Colangelo, owner of both the Phoenix Suns basketball team and the Arizona Diamondbacks, the 2001 World Series Champions. Colangelo has also been ranked by *The Sporting News* as one of the most powerful people in sports for the past ten years.

Mario Gabelli, CEO and chief investment officer of Gabelli Asset Management; Lawrence Auriana, director of the Kaufman Funds; Angelo Mozilo, CEO of Countrywide Credit Industries; and Thomas Marsico, founder and chair of Marsico Funds represent just a few of the Italian-Americans present in the money management and investment sector of the U. S. economy.

Bringing business and market news to the public is Neil Cavuto, the host of Fox news channel's *Your World With Neil Cavuto*, which is the highest-rated business news show on cable. He also coanchors *Cavuto on Business*, and as vice president of *Business News*, he also oversees all business news for Fox. During his twenty years of finan-

Left: Jerry Colangelo, owner of both the Phoenix Suns Basketball team and the Arizona Razorbacks which beat the New York Yankees in the 2001 World Series. (Courtesy of Jerry Colangelo)

Below: Neil Cavuto is Anchor, Managing Editor and Vice-President of Business News for the Fox News Channel. In addition to his top rated "Your World with Neil Cavuto" and his other business shows on Fox, he has written a new best-selling book entitled *More Than Money*. (Courtesy of the Fox News Network)

cial journalism, he has developed a sharp, straightforward, no-nonsense style of interviewing his guests and reporting the news. Yet, he often does it with a good sense of humor and is always "fair and balanced." He has been nominated for five Cable ACE Awards and continually ranked among the most influential business journalists in America. His first book *More Than Money* has made *The New York Times* best-seller list.

Maria Bartiromo is the award winning journalist, host and producer of CNBC's "Special Report with Maria Bartiromo" and co-anchor of "Closing Bell with Maria Bartiromo." (Courtesy of NIAF)

Another influential and trusted business journalist is Maria Bartiromo, host of *Special Report with Maria Bartiromo* and anchor of *Closing Bell with Maria Bartiromo*. Nearly a decade ago Bartiromo was the first journalist to report on a daily basis from the floor of the New York Stock Exchange. Winner of a number of journalism awards, she has been nominated for a Cable ACE Award for her three-part series on the Internet and its implications for investors. Her book *Use the News: How To Separate the Noise From the Investment and Make Money in Any Economy* made several best-seller lists in 2001, including those of *The New York Times* and *The Wall Street Journal.*

The accomplishments of Italians in the political and public life of America came much more gradually than their achievements in other fields. Very few Italians held public office in the United States prior to the 1880s. In fact, only three Italian-Americans—Francis B. Spinola, Anthony J. Caminetti, and Fiorello H. La Guardia—reached national office prior to America's entry into World War I. In 1887 Francis B. Spinola of New York State, a former brigadier-general with the Union Army during the Civil War, became the first Italian-American to be elected to the U. S. House of Representatives. From 1891 to 1895 Anthony J. Caminetti of California served as a member of the U. S. House of Representatives, and in 1913 he was appointed commissioner of immigration by President Woodrow Wilson. In 1900, Andrew Houston Longino was elected governor of Mississippi and strong evidence suggests that Alfred E. Smith, who was elected governor of New York in 1919, was at least on his father's side Italian, making him the first Italian-American governor of New York. His father was Alfred Emanuel Ferrara Smith from Genoa, whose name most likely was changed by a non-Italian immigration officer. Al Smith, of course, who was a Roman Catholic, ran as the Democratic candidate for president of the United States in 1928, losing to Herbert Hoover. The political career of Fiorello H. La Guardia of New York has come to symbolize the beginning of the political maturation of Italian-Americans not only in New York but also in the whole nation. Fiorello H. La Guardia, whose first name means "little flower," was born on Varick Street in New York City on December 11, 1882. His father, Achille, was a southern Italian from Foggia, and his mother, Irene Coen, was a Jew from Trieste. They immigrated to America in 1880, and settled in New York City where Fiorello was born. When Achille joined the Army as a bandmaster in 1882, the family moved to Prescott, Arizona, where Fiorello grew up and received his early education. At the age of sixteen, he moved back to Trieste with his family. At nineteen, he found employment as a clerk in the U.S. consulate in Austria-Hungary; he later became an interpreter at the U. S. consulates in Budapest and Trieste. In 1904 he was appointed U. S. consular agent in Fiume, then in Hungary, but resigned in 1906 and returned to the United States.

In New York City, La Guardia found employment as an interpreter at the Ellis Island Immigration Center, while he studied law at New York University. He received his LL.B. degree in 1910, and took up the practice of law. Five years later he became deputy attorney general for New York and in 1916 was elected to the U. S. House of Representatives as a

Alfred E. Smith, whose grandfather was Alfred Emanuel Ferrara from Genoa, Italy, was the first Italian-American Governor of New York in 1919. (Courtesy of the Library of Congress)

Fiorello H. La Guardia. (Courtesy of the Library of Congress)

Progressive Republican. During World War I he served as a bomber pilot in the United States Air Corps. After the war, he was reelected to the House, but a year later gave up his congressional seat to become president of the New York City Board of Aldermen. In that position he fought graft and corruption in city politics, particularly in the Tammany political machine. In 1922 he was reelected to Congress on the Republican ticket, where he remained until Franklin Roosevelt's political landslide in 1932. While in Congress, he supported legislation that abolished arbitrary injunctions as a weapon for breaking strikes and advocated the repeal of Prohibition. In 1933, La Guardia, running on an anti-Tammany Hall ticket, was elected mayor of New York City, thus becoming the first Italian-American to win such a high public office.

As mayor of New York, La Guardia worked tirelessly against graft and corruption in city government. He balanced the city budget and fostered the development of dozens of community projects such as bridges, parks, schools, hospitals, highways as well as the airport bearing his name. With a flare for the dramatic, he was often seen making rounds with policemen or riding fire trucks. When New York's newspapers once went on strike, he read the comic strips over the radio to children and adults alike. New Yorkers showed their appreciation by reelecting La Guardia in 1937 and again in 1941. He chose not to run for reelection in 1946, due to declining health. In 1946, he became director of the United Nations Relief and Rehabilitation Administration. His poor health again forced him to resign this position after only a few months. On September 20, 1947, he died.

Following in the footsteps of La Guardia, other New York Italian-Americans also played active roles in politics and public life. Edward Corsi, an immigrant from Abruzzi, served as commissioner of immigration from 1931 to 1934 and as industrial commissioner for New York from 1943 to 1955. In 1955 he became assistant U.S. secretary of state. Ferdinand Percora established an outstanding record as legal counsel to the U. S. Committee on Banking and Currency during the 1930s. After serving a term as district attorney in New York City, he was elected justice of the Supreme Court of New York State. Charles Poletti, another outstanding lawyer, was elected lieutenant-governor of New York in 1939. And, for a short period in 1942, when Governor Herbert H. Lehman was elected to the United States Senate, Poletti served as governor. Vito Marcantonio,

Rudolph W. Giuliani served as the 107th Mayor of New York City from 1994–2001. Especially hailed for his calm and effective leadership during the September 11, 2001 terrorist attacks. (Courtesy of the NYC Archives)

a protege of La Guardia, served seven terms in the U. S. House of Representatives. In 1949, he ran for mayor of New York, but was defeated by another Italian-American, Vincent Impelliteri. Mean-while, Carmine De Sapio had gained control of Tammany Hall, where he exercised considerable influence in nominating candidates for city, state, and national office.

After more than three decades, another Italian-American, Rudolph W. Guiliani, was elected as mayor of New York in 1993. Guiliani capitalized on his fame as the U.

S. Attorney for Southern District of New York who successfully prosecuted and convicted drug dealers, organized crime figures, corrupt government officials, and white-collar criminals. In his mayoral campaigns, he stressed anti-crime, pro-business, pro-education, and quality-of-life issues. In a close and bitter election with racial overtones, Guiliani defeated incumbent Mayor David Dinkins. Making good on his campaign promises, Guiliani was reelected as mayor by a wide margin in 1998, winning in four out of five of the

Mario Cuomo served three terms as Governor of New York from 1982 to 1994, and is presently practicing law with Willkie, Farr & Gallagher, while lecturing nationwide on public policy and international issues. (Courtesy of Mario Cuomo)

city's boroughs. It was Mayor Guiliani's steady calm, tenacity, and effective leadership during the terrorist attacks on September 11, 2001 on the World Trade Center that prompted *Time* magazine's choice of him as "Person of the Year" for 2001. It also garnered him an honorary title from Queen Elizabeth II of the United Kingdom.

Mario Matthew Cuomo, the son of an Italian immigrant grocer, was elected governor of New York in 1982. In 1986 and in 1990 he won a second and third four-year term by a high percentage of votes. During his twelve-year tenure as governor, he pursued highly progressive social-service programs for the homeless, the mentally ill, AIDS patients, children's healthcare, and welfare. He worked to improve New York's infrastructure and environment. He vetoed bills on the death penalty, built additional prison space, and enacted the nation's first seatbelt law. In the process it is estimated that he created at least three hundred thousand jobs in New York. He gave a brilliant speech as the keynote speaker at the 1984 Democratic National Convention and was considered a favorite to run for president in 1988 and 1992, but refused to run. Despite his solid record of achievement, Cuomo failed to win a fourth gubernatorial reelection. This was owed, in part, to the Republican revolution in 1994 and to a very strong campaign run by conservative Republican George E. Pataki, whose mother is Italian-

89

American.

Before he was elected governor, George Pataki had been mayor of Peekskill, New York, and a member of the New York state legislature for ten years. As governor, he advocated spending cuts and tax cuts and supported comprehensive healthcare legislation. He was reelected in 1998 and again in 2002, serving as the present governor of New York.

George E. Pataki, Governor of New York. (Courtesy of the Office of Governor Pataki)

Outside of New York, Italian-Americans also gained political prominence. In California, Angelo Rossi became the first Italian-American elected mayor of San Francisco holding that office from 1931 to 1944. Joseph Alioto, a prominent attorney and self-made millionaire, became the second Italian-American elected mayor of San Francisco. He was first elected in 1967 and reelected in 1971. One of the most popular politicians on the West Coast, Alioto could have attained national office if he had been so inclined. Robert S. Maestri served as mayor of New Orleans from 1936 to 1946. Thomas D'Alesandro, Jr., served three terms as mayor of Baltimore from 1947 to 1959. In 1971, Frank Rizzo, a tough but fair "law and order" former police chief was elected mayor of Philadelphia. During the past two decades dozens of other Italian-Americans were elected mayors in cities throughout the country, including Thomas Menino, who was the first Italian-American elected mayor of Boston in 1993.

John O. Pastore of Rhode Island, the son of an immigrant tailor, holds the distinction of being the third Italian-American elected as state governor. In 1950 he also became the first Italian-American elected to the U. S. Senate. Other Italians who served as governors include Christopher Del Sesto and John Notte of Rhode Island; Foster Furcolo and John A. Volpe of Massachusetts; Albert D. Rossellini of Washington; Michael Vincent Di Salle of Ohio; and Ella Grasso of Connecticut. Although only nine Americans of Italian heritage—John O. Pastore of Rhode Island, Peter W. Domenici of

Left: Angelo Rossi, the first Italian-American Mayor of San Francisco. (Courtesy of San Francisco Public Library)

Right: Joseph Alioto, former Mayor of San Francisco. (Courtesy of San Francisco Public Library)

Above left: Frank J. Rizzo, former Mayor of Philadelphia. (Courtesy of the Office of Frank J. Rizzo)

Above right: Thomas D'Alesandro, former Mayor of Baltimore. (Courtesy of the D'Alesandro family)

Left: John O. Pastore of Rhode Island became the first Italian-American to be elected governor of a state as well as the first to be elected to the United States Senate. (Courtesy of the Rhode Island Historical Society)

Above: Ella T. Grasso, former Governor of Connecticut. (Courtesy of the office of the Governor of Connecticut)

Left: Thomas M. Menino, Mayor of Boston. (Courtesy of the Office of Mayor Menino)

Left: U.S. Senator Pete Domenici of New Mexico. (Courtesy of the Office of Senator Domenici)

Right: U.S. Senator Patrick Leahy of Vermont. (Courtesy of the Office of Senator Leahy)

Left: U.S. Senator Mary L. Landrieu of Louisiana. (Courtesy of the Office of Senator Landrieu)

Right: U.S. Senator Michael B. Enzi of Wyoming. (Courtesy of the Office of Senator Enzi)

Above left: Peter J. Rodino, who served nineteen terms as Congressman from New Jersey. He presided over the Judiciary Committee's hearings on the impeachment of Richard Nixon. (Courtesy of the Office of Congressman Rodino)

Above right: U.S. Senator Rick Santorum of Pennsylvania. (Courtesy of the Office of Senator Santorum)

Right: Geraldine Ferraro, Democratic Congresswoman from the state of New York and was the first woman to run for Vice-President of the United States on a major party ticket. (Courtesy of the Global Consulting Group)

New Mexico, Dennis De Concini of Arizona, Patrick Leahy of Vermont, Alphonse D'Amato of New York, Robert Toricelli of New Jersey, Michael Enzi of Wyoming, Mary Landrieu of Louisiana, and Rick Santorum of Pennsylvania—have been elected to the U. S. Senate, numerous Italian-Americans have been elected to the House of Representatives. Peter Rodino of New Jersey, head of the House Judiciary Committee, gained national fame and the respect of the nation for the manner in which he conducted the im-peachment hearings of Richard Nixon in 1974. In 1984,

Congresswoman Nancy Pelosi of California's Eighth District. She was elected in 2002 as the Democratic Leader of the House of Representatives, becoming the first woman in history to lead a major party in the U.S. Congress. (Courtesy of the Office of Representative Pelosi)

Geraldine Ferraro, a former U. S. congresswoman from New York, became the first woman ever to run as a nominee of a major political party for vice president of the United States. In 1987 Nancy Pelosi, the daughter of Thomas D. Alesandro, Jr., who once served as mayor of Baltimore, was elected to represent California's Eighth Congressional District in the House of Representatives. In 2002, after five terms in Congress, she was overwhelmingly elected by her Democratic colleagues in the House as the Democratic Leader, becoming the first woman in American history to head a major party in the U.S. Congress.

Also winning national acclaim for helping to preserve the American system of government in the troubled Watergate period was Judge John Sirica, the son of an

Judge John J. Sirica, who presided in the "Watergate" case. (Courtesy of the Office of Judge J. Sirica)

Italian immigrant from San Volento. As judge in the "Watergate" case, he ruled that the rights and privileges of the presidency absolved the president from surrendering the "tapes" or other evidence if called upon to do so by the court. The first Italian-American cabinet member was Anthony Celebrezze, who served as secretary of health, education, and welfare in the Kennedy and Johnson administrations. Under

Supreme Court Justice Antonin Scalia, first Italian-American named to the Supreme Court of the United States. (Courtesy of the U.S. Supreme Court)

Richard Nixon, John A. Volpe served as secretary of transportation and later, became U.S. ambassador to Italy. President Jimmy Carter named Joseph A. Califano, Jr., secretary of health, education, and welfare and Benjamin Civeletti as attorney general of the United States. In 1986 Antonin Scalia became the first and only Italian-American ever appointed as a justice to the U.S. Supreme Court. Leon Panetta, a former congressman from California, was appointed by President William J. Clinton as the first Italian-American to serve as White House chief of staff. Panetta, who held that position from 1994 to 1997, was succeeded by John Podesta, who also served under President Clinton from 1998 to 2001. Charles O. Rossotti became commissioner of the Internal Revenue Service in 1997, bringing much improved technology as well as better consumer service to the agency.

Nominated by President George W.

Msgr. Geno Baroni. (Courtesy of the Archdiocese of Washington, D.C.)

Left: John Podesta served as Chief of Staff to President William J. Clinton (from 1998 to 2001) and is presently Chief Executive Officer of the Center for American Progress in Washington, D.C. (Courtesy of the Center for American Progress)

Right: Leon Panetta served as Chief of Staff to President William J. Clinton from 1994-1997 and is presently Director of the Leon and Sylvia Panetta Institute for Public Policy in Seaside, California. (Courtesy of the Panetta Institute)

Bush, and confirmed by the U.S. Senate, Anthony J. Principi became secretary of the department of veteran affairs in 2001. It is the second largest department of the federal government with more than 230,000 employees responsible for looking after hundreds of medical centers, benefits offices, and national cemeteries for veterans and their dependents.

Many more Italian-Americans have gained national recognition for their accomplishments in public service. In 1977 President Carter appointed Monsignor Geno Baroni, the son of an immigrant coal miner from Pennsylvania, assistant secretary for neighborhood voluntary associations and consumer protection under H.U.D. Prior to that position, Monsignor Baroni headed the National Center for Urban Ethnic Affairs. This organization has done much to upgrade the status of minorities and ethnic groups in American society. Another Roman Catholic priest, Father James Groppi, had been acknowledged as one of the

Anthony J. Principi is Secretary of Veterans Affairs, responsible for a nationwide system of health care services, benefits, programs and National Cemeteries for America's veterans and their dependents. (Courtesy of the Office of Veteran's Affairs)

leading civil rights activists in the country in the sixties and early seventies.

Bishop Francis J. Mugavero was appointed the first Italian-American Bishop of Brooklyn, New York, in 1968. Known as the "Bishop of Charity," he was instrumental in the establishment of the Catholic Campaign for Human Development and initiated an interfaith program that created hundreds of affordable homes for low-income residents of Brooklyn. Joseph Cardinal Bernardin, son of Italian immigrants and head of Chicago's archdiocese until his death in 1996, was awarded the Presidential Medal of Freedom, the highest honor bestowed on individuals who have made significant contributions to their communities and the nation. In bestowing the medal on Cardinal Bernardin in 1996, President Clinton cited the cardinal for his exemplary efforts in the causes of social justice, racial equality, and arms control. Cardinal Anthony Joseph Bevilacqua and his immediate successor as archbishop of Philadelphia in 2003, Justin Francis Cardinal Rigali, have been charged with the spiritual leadership of more than 1.4 million Roman Catholics in the city of Philadelphia and its surrounding counties. Both prelates have worked very actively in pastoral ministry—visiting

Judge Michael A. Musmanno, a former Pennsylvania Supreme Court Justice and one of the judges who presided at the International Military Trials of War Crimes at Nurenburg in Germany. (Courtesy of Duquesne University)

schools, parishes, prisons, and hospitals, and have championed the cause of social justice.

In the legal profession, Melvin Belli has gained such an international reputation that he is referred to as the "king of torts." Judge Michael A. Musmanno, a Pennsylvania supreme court judge from 1952 to 1968, was appointed by President Kennedy in 1961 to the Commission of International Rules of Judicial Procedure. Musmanno also held the distinction of being one of the presiding judges at the International War Crimes Trial in Nuremberg following World War II. Frank C. Carlucci served as U. S. ambassador to

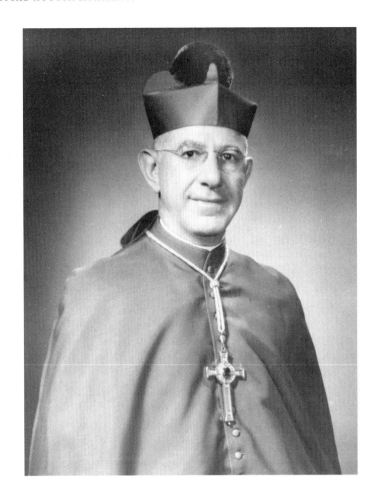

Above left: Cardinal Justin Francis Rigali, Archbishop of Philadelphia, is the spiritual leader of more than 1.4 million Catholics. (Courtesy of the Archdiocese of Philadelphia)

Above right: Bishop Francis J. Mugavero was the first Brooklyn-born Italian-American to become Bishop of the Diocese of Brooklyn. Known as "the Bishop of Charity," he was instrumental in establishing the Catholic Bishop's Catholic Campaign for Human Development. (Courtesy of the Roman Catholic Diocese of Brooklyn)

Bottom right: Melvin Belli, internationally known trial lawyer referred to as the "King of Torts." (Courtesy of the Law Offices of Belli and Choulos)

Joseph Cardinal Bernadin, late Archbishop of Chicago, receiving the Presidential Medal of Freedom, the highest civilian honor bestowed on citizens, from President Clinton for his dedication to racial equality, arms control and social justice. (White House Photo, Courtesy of NIAF)

Bottom left: General Peter Pace is Vice-Chairman of the Joint Chiefs of Staff, the Nation's second highest ranking military officer and the first Marine to hold that position. (Courtesy of the Office of Joint Chiefs of Staff)

Bottom right: Frank Carlucci, Secretary of Defense in President Ronald Reagan's Administration. (Courtesy of the Office of Deputy Secretary of Defense)

Portugal from 1975 to 1978, deputy director of the Central Intelligence Agency from 1978 to 1980, and in 1980, became deputy secretary of defense.

In 2001 highly decorated Marine General Peter Pace was promoted to vice chairman of the joint chiefs of staff. General Pace is the sixth officer to hold the nation's second highest military rank and the first marine. Among his personal decorations are the Bronze Star for Combat, the Defense Distinguished Service Medal, and the Legion of Merit.

William Novelli is Chief Executive Officer of the AARP with a membership of over 35 million people age 50 and older. (Courtesy of the AARP Executive Office)

William D. Novelli is the current CEO of the AARP, a membership organization of more than 35 million Americans aged 50 and older. As the head of the AARP, he has been a major advocate of programs and legislation that benefit America's senior citizens. The list of lesser-known Italian-Americans in political and public life runs into the thousands. Their accomplishments have also made significant contributions to American life.

CHAPTER FIVE

CONTRIBUTIONS
IN EVERY FIELD

T he more than five million Italians who came to America in search of a better life have, in the process of their quest, made an enormous contribution to American society. In the arts, sciences, and humanities Italian-Americans have enriched the cultural and social life of America. On the battlefield they demonstrated their loyalty, courage, and patriotism in defense of the United States. In the field of sports they have excited, thrilled, and entertained millions of Americans.

Undoubtedly, the most obvious contributions of Italians to the cultural life of America have come from those in the performing arts. Since colonial days, Italian musicians, singers, actors, actresses, and dancers have performed in America. Lorenzo Da Ponte, who arrived in the United States from Italy in 1805, was probably the man most responsible for popularizing opera in America. For over thirty years of his life Da Ponte tirelessly promoted the importing of Italian opera companies to the United States. In 1833 his enterprising efforts resulted in the first opera house being built in the country. During the course of the nineteenth century Italian opera singers and their companies toured from the East Coast to the West. Adelina Patti, the very talented coloratura soprano, made debuts in New York, New Orleans,

Lorenzo da Ponte, who was most responsible for promoting opera in America during the early days of our Republic. (Courtesy of Columbia University in the City of New York)

The legendary opera star Enrico Caruso. (Courtesy of the Library of Congress)

Italian Luciano Pavarotti is not only one of the great opera stars of all time, but has remained one of the most popular celebrities in America. (Courtesy of David Town; London Records)

and San Francisco by the end of the century. The great Metropolitan Opera House of New York City opened on October 22, 1883.

The Neapolitan-born Enrico Caruso made his debut at the Metropolitan Opera House in 1903. His magnificent performances in such operas as *Carmen*, *Pagliacci*, and *Aida* soon established him as the most popular tenor in the country. His seventeen-year association and more than six hundred performances at the Metropolitan not only thrilled his audiences but also established a golden age of opera in America. Opera audiences come to hear the Italian voices of Antonio Scotti, Alessandro Bonci, Giovanni Martinelli, Luisa Tetrazzini, Tita Roffo, Claudia Muzzio, and Lina Cavalieri. More recently, Licia Albanese, Richard Bonelli, Cesare Sepi, Renata Tebaldi, Anna Moffo, Carmela and Rosa Ponselle, Mario Lanza, Ezio Pinza, Marguerite Piazza, Luciano Pavarotti, and many others have delighted American opera fans everywhere. Several of these opera stars, including Ezio Pinza and Mario Lanza, have also appeared in stage and movie musicals. Luciano Pavarotti is not only one of the great opera stars of today, but he has become one of the most popular celebrities in America due to the success of his records, his best-selling autobiography, and his numerous appearances on television.

Left: Mario Lanza, opera and film star. (Courtesy of RCA Records)

Right: Adelina Patti, one of the most outstanding opera stars of the late nineteenth century. (Courtesy of the New York Public Library at Lincoln Center)

Above left: Licia Albanese, opera star. (Courtesy of the Puccini Foundation)

Above right: Luisa Tetrazzini, one of the great opera stars of the twentieth century. (Courtesy of the New York Public Library at Lincoln Center)

Arturo Toscanini, undoubtedly the most famous symphony conductor of the twentieth century. (Courtesy of the Library of Congress)

Music critics still acclaim Arturo Toscanini as the greatest operatic and orchestral conductor of the twentieth century. Born in Parma, Italy, in 1867, Toscanini began his musical career as a cellist. While on tour with an Italian orchestra in Rio de Janeiro in Brazil, Toscanini made his spectacular debut as a conductor when the local conductor was unable to perform. Returning to Italy, he gained an outstanding reputation for conducting at La Scala Opera in Milan. In 1908 Toscanini made his debut at the Metropolitan Opera House in New York. Music critics immediately proclaimed him the "epitome of musicianship" and the "greatest musical interpreter" of the times. After six years of conducting at the Metropolitan, he returned to Italy. After World War I he again took over as conductor at La Scala. Coming into disfavor with Benito Mussolini and the Fascists, Toscanini

Left: Dominick Argento, Pulitzer Prize winning composer. (Courtesy of Boosey and Hawkes)

Right: David Del Tredici, Pulitzer Prize winning composer. (Photo by Jack Mitchell— Courtesy of Boosey and Hawkes)

resigned his position at La Scala and ventured again to New York. In 1929 he became the principal conductor of the New York Philharmonic, where his brilliant interpretations of Italian and German composers brought him enormous fame. In 1937 he became conductor of the NBC Symphony Orchestra where, through newly developed high-quality radio receivers and recordings, millions of Americans came to appreciate his music. After sixteen years of touring and recording with the NBC symphony, he returned to Italy where he died in 1951.

Gian Carlo Menotti, a Pulitzer Prize winning composer. (Courtesy of the New York Public Library at Lincoln Center)

Among the Pulitzer-Prize winning Italian-American composers are Gian Carlo Menotti, Walter Piston, David Del Tredici, and John Corigliano. Corigliano who won the Pulitzer Prize for his *Symphony No 2* in 2001 is internationally acclaimed for his orchestral chamber, opera, and film work. In 2000 he won an Academy Award for his film score *The Red Violin*. Guy and Carmen Lombardo, Henry Mancini, Ralph Marterie, Frankie Carle, and Carmen Cavallaro have been among the most renowned of the orchestral leaders in the history of popular music in America. For many years Joe Venuti, James La Rocca, Leon Rappallo, and Joe Marsala headed a list of notable jazz performers. More recently, Chuck Mangione has come to be ranked among the top jazz musicians and composers in America. In the field of popular dance, Peter Gennaro remains one of the most respected dancers and choreographers. Another Italian-American, Matteo has distinguished himself in the field of ethnic dance and serves as the artistic director of his own dance theater in New York City. Jose Greco, a native of Abruzzi, did much to popularize Spanish dancing in America.

John Corigliano, winner of the 2001 Pulitzer Prize in Music for his "Symphony No. 2" is internationally celebrated by many music critics as one of the leading composers of the twenty-first century. (Courtesy of Fine Arts Management)

Guy Lombardo remembered for the "sweetest music this side of heaven" and New Years Eve celebrations. (Courtesy of the Guy Lombardo Orchestra)

Generally regarded as one of, if not the, greatest, male vocalists of our time was Frank Sinatra. His singing career spanned six decades and his list of hit records, live performances, television specials, and movies made Sinatra something of an entertainment institution in America. Other Italian-American male vocalists who have enjoyed considerable popularity and success are Russ Colombo, Perry Como, Dean Martin, Tony Bennett, Vic Damone, Frankie Lane, Jerry Vale, Enzo Stuarti, Al Martino, and Julius La Rosa. Among the most popular Italian-American female vocalists are Liza Minnelli, Connie Francis, Joni James, Annette Funicello, Kaye Ballard, Anna Maria Alberghetti, and Carol Lawrence. Bringing laughter to millions of Americans have been Italian-American comedians such as Lou Costello, Jimmy Durante, Jerry Colonna, Jimmy Savo, Judy Canova, Norm Crosby, Dom DeLuise, and Pat Cooper.

From Rudolph Valentino, the romantic movie idol of the 1920s, hundreds of actors and actresses of Italian heritage have distinguished themselves in the theater, movies, and television. Just a few of the more notable are Burt Reynolds, Frank Sinatra, Al Pacino, Ernest Borgnine, Rossano Brazzi, Ann Brancroft, Liza Minnelli, Alan Alda, Dean Martin, Harry Guardino, James Coco, James Farentino, Ben Gazzara, Anthony Franciosa, Don Ameche, Sergio Franchi, Sylvester Stallone, Tony Danza, Ida Lupino,

Henry Mancini, who received 15 Academy Award nominations and three of the coveted Oscars for his motion picture scores and songs, and has also garnered 20 Grammy Awards and 6 Gold Albums for his music. (Courtesy of Shanoson and Schwam)

Anita Gillette, Brenda Vaccaro, Frank Langella, Diane Civita, John Travolta, Al Molinaro, Valerie Bertinelli, Madonna, Danny De Vito, Ray Romano, Angelica Hueston, Leonardo di Caprio, Paul Sorvino, Mira Sorvino, Nicholas Cage, James Gandolfini, Edie Falco, Joe

108

Left: Chuck Mangione, a leading jazz musician and composer in America today. (Courtesy of Gates Music, Inc.)

Right: Peter Gennaro, one of the most highly reputed dancers and choreographers in America. (Courtesy of Peter Gennaro)

Below left: Perry Como, singer and entertainer. (Courtesy of RCA Records)

Below right: Dean Martin, star of films, television, and records and one of the great entertainers in contemporary America. (Courtesy of Dean Martin Enterprises)

Frank Sinatra, truly one of the greatest entertainers in American History. (Courtesy of Solters, Roskin, Friedman, Inc.)

Left: Tony Bennett, one of the most popular song stylists and entertainers in the twentieth century. (Courtesy of Tony Bennett Enterprises)

Right: Liza Minnelli, superstar of stage, screen, television, and recordings. (Courtesy of Cinemobilia)

Above left: Pat Cooper, a successful comedian, who manages to bring joy and laughter to all in his presence. (Courtesy of Pat Cooper)

Above right: Connie Francis (Concetta Rosemarie Franconlro) top female vocalist of the late 50s and early 60s and among the best female vocalists of all time. (Courtesy of NIAF)

111

Left: Jimmy Savo, ace pantomine-comedian. (Courtesy of Tal Kanigher)

Right: Lou Costello, one of the greatest slapstick comedians of the twentieth century. (Courtesy of Tal Kanigher)

Above left: Comedian Dom DeLuise, who has the talent to put a smile on peoples' faces whenever he appears. (Courtesy of Dom DeLuise)

Above right: Jimmy Durante, "the Schnozz" as he was called by his friends, was one of the greatest entertainers of the twentieth century. (Courtesy of Margie Durante)

Pesci, Christina Ricci, Connie Francis, Chazz Palminteri, Vincent D'Onofrio, Danny Aiello, Ray Liotta, Joe Montegna, and Ben Gazzara. Another Italian-American, Jack Valenti, served for many years as president of the Motion Picture Association until his resignation in 2004. He also held a position as special assistant to President Lyndon Johnson from 1964 to 1968.

Frank Capra, a Sicilian immigrant who came to the United States in 1903 at the age of six, became one of the most successful film directors of the 1930s and 1940s. Stressing themes of good over evil in his films, he won Academy Awards for *It Happened One Night* in 1934, *Mr. Deeds Goes to Town* in 1936, and *You Can't Take It With You* in 1938. He garnered a fourth Oscar for best documentary for his *Prelude to War* in 1942 as part of the U.S. Army documentary series during World War II.

In the post World War II-era a new generation of Italian-American filmmakers emerged. Francis Ford Coppola, Michael Cimino, Brian De Palma, Vincent Minelli, and Martin Scorsese have all made their mark as directors in the annals of American film history. Coppola, a daring innovator as a filmmaker, who met with little success with his early films, struck cinematic and financial success with *The Godfather* (based on Mario Puzo's novel) in 1972, and *Godfather II* in 1974, the former winning an Oscar for best picture and the latter taking seven Oscars. Coppola captured three of those for best picture, best screen play, and best director. *The Deer Hunter* in 1978 was Michael Cimino's most successful film, winning five Academy Awards, including best director. Brian De Palma, known for his bizzare storytelling, special effects, and graphic violence has given us such films as *Obsession* in 1976, *Carrie* in 1976, *The Fury* in 1978, *Dressed to Kill* in 1980, and

Rudolph Valentino, the idol of the American cinema of the 1920s. (Courtesy of the Library of Congress)

113

Above left: Academy Award winning actor Ernest Borgnine. (Courtesy of Ernest Borgnine)

Above right: Al Pacino, one of the greatest actors in film history, often nominated for Academy Awards and winning the Oscar for Best Actor for his performance in "Scent of a Woman." (Courtesy of NIAF)

Left: James Coco, comedian and accomplished actor. (Courtesy of Paul H. Wolfowitz)

Right: Alan Alda, baptized Alphonzo D'Abruzzo, overcame polio as a child to become a superstar in television and movies, especially noted for his starring role in "MASH." (Courtesy of WDAU-TV in Scranton—CBS Affiliated Station)

Left: Sylvester Stallone, actor, writer, producer and director who is best known for his Academy Award winning film, "Rocky." (Courtesy of Herbert Nanas Organization)

Right: Frank Langella Jr., an actor best known for his role in "Dracula." (Courtesy of Frank A. Langella Sr.)

Above left: Paul Sorvino, veteran actor, opera singer, painter and sculptor, holds an honorary doctorate from the University of Scranton. He is also the father of Academy Award winning actress Mira Sorvino. (Courtesy of the University of Scranton)

Above right: Ray Romano stars as Ray Barone on "Everybody Loves Raymond." (Photo cr: Monty Briton—Courtesy of CBS)

115

Left: Frank Capra, with sun glasses, and colleague directing one of the films that garnered him several Academy Awards. (Courtesy of New York Public Library at Lincoln Center)

Right: Jack Valenti, President of the Motion Picture Association of America for nearly three decades before his recent retirement. (Courtesy of the Motion Picture Association of America, Inc.)

Above left: James Gandolfini and Eddie Falco, both accomplished award winning actors, co-starring in the hit HBO drama series *The Sopranos*. (Photo cr: Karambouris—Courtesy of WireImage)

Above right: Jon Bon Jovi (John Francis Bongiovi, Jr.), actor and musician, who has enjoyed more than 20 years of success as a rock star winning numerous accolades and awards. (Courtesy of NIAF)

Frank Zappa, one of the most original exotic and complex figures to emerge from the Rock Culture of the 1960s, recorded more than 50 albums, before he succumbed to cancer at the age of 52. (Courtesy of Greg Gorman Photography, Los Angeles, California)

Madonna (Madonna Louise Ciccone) one of the most innovative and controversial music icons of our era, interviewed by fellow Italian-American Jay Leno, outstanding night club comedian and star of the *Tonite Show* since 1992. (Photo cr. Drinkwater— Courtesy of WireImage)

Blow Out in 1981.

Also, a part of the new generation of filmmakers in the 1970s and 1980s, Martin Scorsese is one of the most prolific filmmakers in the history of American cinema. Born in Queens, New York, in 1942, Scorsese spent much of his youth in Manhattan's Little Italy. As a child he suffered from asthma, which restricted his physical activities but led him to spend a considerable amount of time at the movies. Reared in a devout Roman Catholic family, he stud-

Three of the remarkable Coppolas, all of whom have won Academy Awards actor Nicholas Cage (Nicholas Kim Coppola), his cousin Sophia, actress, director and screenwriter and her father Francis Ford Coppola, renowned director and now accomplished vitner. (Photo cr. Vespa—Courtesy of WireImage)

ied briefly for the priesthood before entering New York University's film school. There he earned a master's degree and taught film courses for several years.

Drawing on his personal experiences in Little Italy, Scorsese's first feature length film *Who's That Knocking at My Door* in 1968 tells the story of a young Italian-American man confronted with life on the tough streets of his neighborhood. After making several documentaries in the early 1970s, dealing with such subjects as the anti-war movement and the counter culture, he made *Mean Streets* in 1973 about a young man trying to raise himself out of the ghetto of Little Italy. It features a young actor, Robert De Niro, with whom Scorsese has had a collaborative relationship throughout his career. Additional film successes came with *Alice Doesn't Live Here Anymore* in 1975, *Taxi Driver* in 1976, *New York, New York* in 1977, *Raging Bull* in 1980, and *King of Comedy* in 1983. *The Color of Money* in 1986 was a big box-office hit followed by the controversial *The Last Temptation of Christ* in 1988. His mob masterpiece *Goodfellas* came in 1990 followed by another gangster film *Casino* in 1995. In the meantime he made a series of other films including *Cape Fear* in 1991, *The Age of Innocence* in 1993, *Kundun* in 1997, and *Bringing Out the Dead* in 1999.

Martin Scorsese, a renowned filmmaker whose work has virtually redefined the American Cinema in the last decade of the twentieth century. (Courtesy of PMK)

Scorsese's first major film of the twenty-first century was *Gangs of New York*, a powerful drama about New York gangs during the era of the American Civil War. Released in 2002, it was nominated for several Academy Awards but did not take home any Oscars. Most recently, *The Aviator*, *You Can Count on Me*, and an animated film, *Shark Tale* in 2004 have brought Scorsese's resumé up-to-date. Through his award-winning career (he has won more than fifty major awards for his filmmaking)

Joe DiMaggio, one of the greatest baseball players of all time, and a most successful business executive. (Courtesy of Mr. Coffee)

Martin Scorsese has come to be truly revered as a consummate storyteller who has developed a personal style of filmmaking that has made him one of the most innovative and influential film directors of all time.

In the world of sports, Italian-Americans have also succeeded. Baseball, football, and boxing are replete with Italian names. Among the most famous baseball play-

Left: Tommy Lasorda managed the L.A. Dodgers to nearly 1600 regular season wins in 21 seasons, including 2 World Series titles in 4 appearances. (Courtesy of the National Italian-American Sports Hall of Fame)

Right: Yogi Berra, Baseball Hall of Famer and former coach of the New York Yankees. (Courtesy of the New York Yankees)

ers of Italian descent are Joe Di Maggio, Anthony Michael Lazzeri, Yogi Berra, Phil Rizzuto, Frank Crosetti, Cookie Lavagetto, Al Gionfriddo, Vic Raschi, Billy Martin, Dolf Camilli, Sal Bando, Joe Pepitone, Mike Mussina, Dave Righetti, and Mike Piazza. A good number of baseball writers and fans would argue that Joe Di Maggio, "The Yankee Clipper," is the greatest player in the history of the game. Baseball managers Tommy Lasorda of the Los Angeles Dodgers and Joe Torre of the New York Yankees led their respective teams to World Series championships.

    In professional football, Coach Vince Lombardi of the Green Bay Packers holds the enviable record of winning six Western Divisions and five

Sal Bando, star of the Milwaukee Brewers. (Courtesy of Terrace Sporting Goods)

121

Left: Craig Biggio is the star catcher/ second baseman with the Houston Astros who stole over 50 bases in one season. (Photo cr. Ron Vesely— Courtesy of MLB Photos)

Right: Mike Piazza is the star player with the New York Mets who has played in the All Star Game for ten consecutive seasons. (Photo cr. John Grieshop— Courtesy of MLB Photos)

National Championships, including the first Super Bowl. Joe Paterno of the Penn State Nittany Lions remains one of the winningest coaches in college football. Among the countless number of outstanding Italian-American college and professional football players have been Joe Bellino of Navy, Joe Savoldi of Notre Dame, Nick Buoniconti and Dan Marino of the Miami Dolphins, Gino Marchetti of the Baltimore Colts, Andy Robustelli of the New York Giants, John Cappelletti of the Los Angeles Rams, Dan Pastorini of the Houston Oilers, Vince Ferragamo of the Montreal Alouettes, Franco Harris of the Pittsburgh Steelers, and Joe Montana of the San Francisco 49ers. Men's college basketball coaches Rick Patino, Rollie Massimino, and Jimmy Valvano rank among the greatest in collegiate basketball history.

Boxing's Rocky Marciano has become a legend of the ring—retiring in 1956—as the undefeated heavyweight champion of the world with forty-nine victories, forty-three of which were by knockout. Other Italian-Americans holding world boxing titles in various divisions were Primo Carnera, Rocky Graziano, Tony Canzonieri, Carmen Bisilio, Petey Scalzo, Tony De Marco, Willie Pep, Joey Maxim, William Pastrano, Joe and Vince Dundee, and Pete Herman.

Left: Andy Robustelli, one of the all time great football stars of the New York Giants. (Courtesy of the New York Giants)

Right: John Cappelletti, Heisman Trophy winner at Penn State, and outstanding professional football player. (Courtesy of John Cappelletti Associates)

Vince Lombardi, the legendary coach of the Green Bay Packers. (Photo by Vernon J. Biever—Courtesy of the Green Bay Packers)

Left: Joe Bellino of Navy, one of the most outstanding halfbacks to play college football. (Courtesy of the Director of Sports Information at the U.S. Naval Academy)

Right: Joe Savoldi, one of the greatest football players in Notre Dame History. (Courtesy of the Notre Dame Sports Information Department)

Above left: Joe Montana was the only Quarterback to win four NFL titles in four appearances and the only player to win three Super Bowl MVP awards. He began his professional career with the San Francisco 49ers and finished it out with the Kansas City Chiefs. (Courtesy of NIAF)

Above right: Dan Marino, the Miami Dolphins quarterback whose 60,000 yard passes and 400 touchdown passes has made him an NFL legend. (Courtesy of Dan Marino)

Joe Paterno led Penn State to four undefeated
seasons and two National Championships in
1982 and 1986. His 20 wins in 30 Bowl Games
gives him the most victories in the history of
1-A college football. (Courtesy of Penn State
Athletic Office)

Rick Patino, the Head Basketball Coach at the
University of Louisville, is one of the most
accomplished coaches in collegiate basketball
history with over 400 victories. (Courtesy of the
University of Louisville)

Jim Valvano, known as
"Jimmy Vee" led North
Carolina State to the NCAA
National Championship in
1983, died at the age of 47
after a year-long battle with
cancer. (Courtesy of the
News and Observer, Raleigh,
North Carolina)

Above left: The National Italian-American Sports Hall of Fame in Chicago, Illinois enshrined over two hundred Italian-American Champions of sports. (Courtesy of NIASHF)

Above right: Rocky Graziano, outstanding welterweight contender and former Middleweight Champion of the World. (Courtesy of Joseph DeMichele)

Above left: Rocky Marciano, retired undefeated World's Heavyweight Champion. (Courtesy of the *Scranton Times* in Scranton, Pennsylvania)

Above right: Willie Pep, revealing his form as the Featherweight Champion of the World. (Courtesy of the *Scranton Times* in Scranton, Pennsylvania)

Sons of Italian immigrants have also scored well in the sport of golf. Gene Sarazen once won both the British Open and the U. S. Open in the same year. Will Turnesa, Vic Chezzi, Johnny Revolta, Tony Manero, and Ken Venturi have won some of the most coveted championships in the field of golf. In horse racing, Eddie Arcaro, at the time of his retirement, has topped all jockeys in winning mounts and money earnings in the history of the "sport of kings" in America. Three Italian-Americans have won the Indianapolis 500 motor race—Ralph De Palma, Peter De Paolo, and Mario Andretti. Bruno Sammartino held the professional World Champion-ship of Wrestling from 1963 to 1975. Figure skater Linda Fratianne won the first of her four consecutive U. S. cham-pionships when was only fifteen years old. She won the World Championship in 1977 and again in 1979 before winning the silver medal in the 1980 Olympics. She then became a professional, starring with Walt Disney World On Ice. Skater Brian Boitano won four consecutive U. S. championships beginning in 1985, world championships in 1986 and 1988, and the Olympic Gold Medal in 1988. He was the first skater ever to land the triple axle. Mary Lou Retton gained international fame at the 1984 Olympics where she became

Enrico "Hank" Marino, who came to America from Palermo at the age of eleven, holds the distinction of being named the "Bowler of the Half-Century" by the American Bowling Congress. (Courtesy of the American Bowling Congress)

Andy Varipapa, who bowled both left and right handed, was the first bowler ever elected to the Italian-American Sports Hall of Fame and was elected to the ABC Hall of Fame in 1957. (Courtesy of the American Bowling Congress)

Left: Brian Boitano gave one of the cleanest performances in Olympic Skating history to win the Gold Medal in 1988 and has since enjoyed an outstanding professional skating career. (Courtesy of NIASHF)

Right: Linda Fratianne, a spectacular skater known for remarkable spins and triple jumps, she won four U.S. Championships and the Silver Medal in the 1980 Olympics. (Courtesy of the World Figure Skating Museum, Colorado Springs, Colorado)

Above left: Mary Lou Retton won international fame at the 1984 Olympics by becoming the first American woman to win the Gold Medal in All-Around women's gymnastics. (Photo cr. Meyer—Courtesy of WireImage)

Above right: Matt Biondi, the swimmer who captured eleven medals including eight gold during the course of his Olympic career. (Courtesy of NIASHF)

Left: Gene Sarazen, winner of both the British and the United States Golf Opens in the same year. (Courtesy of *The Scranton Times* in Scranton, Pennsylvania)

Right: Phil Esposito, hockey great of the New York Rangers. (Courtesy of the New York Rangers)

Above left: Willie Mosconi, a world champion in the field of pocket billiards. (Courtesy of Willie Mosconi)

Above right: Mario Andretti, world champion race car driver. (Courtesy of Mario Andretti)

the first American women ever to win the gold medal in the all-around in women's gymnastics. She was inducted into the U. S. Gymnastics Hall of Fame in 1985 and the International Gymnastics Hall Fame in 1997. For over a decade, she has hosted the Children's Miracle Network Celebration television broadcast. Matt Biondi, Olympic swimmer, swam in the 1984, 1988, 1992, and 1996 Olympics and won eleven medals, five of which were gold. The legendary Willie Mosconi in the sport of pocket billiards; Andy Varipapa, Hank Marino, and Frank Santore in bowling; and, the Esposito brothers in the field of hockey are just a few of the hundreds of Italian-Americans who have achieved fame in sports.

Eddie Arcaro undoubtedly the greatest jockey of the twentieth century, winning the Kentucky Derby five times and the Preakness and Belmont each six times. (Courtesy of Donald Grey)

Jennifer Capriati, at the age of 14, was the youngest Grand Slam semifinalist ever and today she remains one of the top ranking tennis players in the world (Photo by Michael Baz— Courtesy of IMG)

From the sportsfield to the battlefield, Italians have made a substantial contribution to America. Nearly two hundred thousand Italian-Americans served in the U. S. armed forces during World War I. Two were awarded the Congressional Medal of Honor for their bravery and heroism. About one hundred received distinguished service crosses, while thousands of other Italian-Americans made up the list of war casualties. More than five hundred thousand Italian-Americans served in the armed forces of this country in World War II. Of those decorated for their valor and gallantry, thirteen received the Congressional Medal of Honor and ten were cited with the Navy Cross. Among those so honored was Marine Gunnery Sergeant John Basilone of New Jersey, whom General MacArthur called a "one man army" and who was awarded the Medal of Honor for his bravery at Guadacanal. He was later killed in the battle of Iwo Jima.

Another Italian-American medal of honor winner was Gino J. Merli of Pennsylvania. While serving as a machine gunner with the 18th Infantry near Sars la Bruyer, Belgium, on the night of September 4, 1944, Private Merli's company was attacked by a superior German force. He found himself surrounded by enemy troops. Over and over again throughout the night of September 4, the enemy stormed his position. On two occasions he feigned dead only to regain his position and continue his fire on the enemy. On the morning of September 5, there were "fifty-two enemy dead, nineteen of whom were in front of his gun."

An Italian scientific genius who contributed to the U. S. victory over Japan in World War II was Enrico Fermi, "the father of the atomic bomb." This remarkable Roman-born physicist had received the Nobel

Marine Gunnery Sergeant John Basilone, who was awarded the Congressional Medal of Honor for his heroism at Guadalcanal in 1942 and killed in action at the Battle of Iwo Jima in 1945, being awarded posthumously the Navy Cross. (Courtesy of the United States Marine Corps)

Private First Class Gino J. Merli, who was awarded the Congressional Medal of Honor for his bravery and courage shown in a battle against superior German forces on the night of September 4, 1944, in Sars La Bruyere, Belgium. (Courtesy of Gino J. Merli)

Prize in Physics in 1938 for his "identification of new radioactive elements produced by neutron bombardment and his discovery made in connection with his work of nuclear reactions effected by slow neutrons." The following year Fermi, being Jewish and disillusioned with the Fascist regime in Italy, immigrated to the United States. He became professor of physics at Columbia University, where he worked continuously on his experiments in nuclear fission. In 1942 Fermi left New York for Chicago, where he joined other renowned scientists in developing the first sustaining chain reaction which permitted the controlled release of nuclear energy—the basis for the atomic bomb had been achieved. After he had completed his work on the so-called "Manhattan Project," which produced the atomic bombs dropped on Japan in World War II, Fermi accepted a professorship of physics at the University of Chicago, where he continued his research until his death in 1954.

A fellow Italian-born physicist and professor of physics at the University of California, Emilio Segre, shared the Nobel Prize in Physics with Professor Owen Chamberlain for demonstrating the existence of the subatomic particle called antiproton. This work resulted in a big step in research into the nature and construction of the universe. Salvatore Luria, another Italian immigrant to America, won the Nobel Prize in the field of Physiology or Medicine in 1969. In 1986, Rita Levi-Montalcini shared the Nobel Prize in Physiology or Medicine with her former student Stanley Cohen for their discovery of the factor that promoted growth of cells in the peripheral nervous system. A native of Turin, Italy, Rita Levi-Montalcini became a U.S. citizen in 1956. Dr. Louis Ignarro was named a Nobel laureate in 1998 for his groundbreaking research on nitric oxide. He developed a formulation of ingredients based on cellular nutrition that optimizes the production of health-enhancing nitric oxide in the body. Dr. Ignarro also received the Basic Research Prize of the American Heart Association for his study that advanced the study of cardiovascular science.

Fifty years after Giuseppe Bellanca, an Italian immigrant aviation pioneer, had flown the first cabin aircraft across the Atlantic Ocean, Rocco Anthony Petrone, the son of an Italian immigrant, played a major role in NASA's launching of the Moon Project. In March 2002, another Italian-American, Astronaut Michael J. Massimino flew on the STS-109 servicing mission that successfully upgraded the Hubble Space Telescope.

Left: Enrico Fermi, winner of the Nobel Prize in Physics. (Courtesy of the Argonne National Library)

Right: Emilio Segre awarded the Nobel Prize in Physics for demonstrating the existence of the sub-atomic particle called the anti-proton. (Courtesy of Emilio Segre)

Above left: Rita Levi-Montalcini received the Nobel Prize in Physiology in 1986 for describing how tumors can affect nerve growths. (© The Nobel Foundation—Courtesy of The Nobel Foundation)

Above right: Salvatore E. Luria, awarded the Nobel Prize in Physiology and Medicine, and is presently Director of the Center for Cancer Research at the Massachusetts Institute of Technology. (Courtesy of the Massachusetts Institute of Technology)

Guiseppe Bellanca with his hand on the propeller of the "Bellanca Parasol," which he designed and built during the early days of aviation. This plane had just one seat and a 30 HP Anzani engine and students were taught to fly it with the aid of a throttle limiter, which initially allowed only brief hops. (Courtesy of the Smithsonian Institution)

Left: Astronaut Michael Massimino, Ph.D. flew on STS-109 Columbia, logging 10 days in space, including 2 space-walks totaling 13 hours and 46 minutes. (Courtesy of NASA)

Right: Rocco Petrone, Director of the Apollo program which put a man on the moon. (Courtesy of NASA)

During the mission, Massimino logged more than ten days in space, including two space-walks, totaling fourteen hours and forty-six minutes. He presently serves as a spacecraft communicator at NASA's Mission Control at the Lyndon B. Johnson Space Center in Houston, Texas. Thousands of Italian-American scientists in every field serve on university faculties. Thousands more conduct scientific research in various departments of government as well as in the laboratories of private companies and corporations.

A. Bartlett Giamatti appointed one of the youngest Presidents of Yale University in 1978, at the age of 40. He went on to become Commissioner of Major league Baseball in 1989 just before his untimely death. (Courtesy of NIAF)

Hundreds of Italian-Americans have served as college presidents. Dr. Peter Sammartino, along with his wife, Sally, founded Fairleigh Dickinson in 1942. In that year he raised $60,000 to purchase a building and recruited sixty students. At the end of the first quarter century and during the first twenty-five years of his presidency, Fairleigh Dickinson University was a seven-campus university with seventy-five buildings and an enrollment of twenty thousand students. Today it remains one of the largest private institutions in the United States. A. Bartlett Giamatti, appointed one of the youngest presidents of Yale University in 1978, at the age of 40, is credited with helping Yale recover from its economic difficulties in the 1970s. An avid baseball fan, he later became president of the National League in 1986 and then commissioner of Major League

Dr. and Mrs. Peter Sammartino, the founders of Fairleigh Dickinson University in New Jersey. Dr. Peter Sammartino was Chancellor and President of Fairleigh Dickinson. (Courtesy of Fairleigh Dickinson University)

Baseball in 1989. In that capacity he oversaw the banishment of baseball superstar Pete Rose from Major League Baseball and the possibility of Rose entering the Hall of Fame because of his gambling on the sport.

Throughout the United States, tens of thousands of Italian-American doctors, dentists, and other medical professionals have performed immeasurable services and deeds that have benefited American society. Even before World War II, Italian-Americans began to influence the field of medicine. In the 1930s Vincent Ciccone developed several methods of mass-producing penicillin as well as having invented the

Left: Edmund Pellegrino, M.D., authored or coauthored nineteen books and over 550 articles in the field of medical science and ethics. (Courtesy of the Center for Bioethics and Human Dignity)

Right: Louis J. Ingarro, M.D., winner of the Nobel Prize in Medicine for his discovery concerning nitric oxide as a signaling molecule in the cardiovascular system. (Courtesy of Dr. Louis J. Ingarro)

cough drop. During his fifty-year career in the medical profession, Edmund Pellegrino, M.D., presently professor emeritus at the Georgetown Medical Center, is one of the leading experts in the field of medicine in the United States, having authored or coauthored nineteen books and more than 550 articles in medicine, philosophy, and ethics. Louis Lasagna, M.D., known as the "Sigmund Freud of Clinical Pharmacology," was a pioneer in the field of drug evaluation. In 1954 he published one of the first scientific articles demonstrating the "placebo effect" on patients. Robert C. Gallo, M.D. founder and director of the Institute of Human Virology at the University of Maryland Biotechnical Institute codiscovered with Dr. Luc Montagnier from Queens College in

Left: Louis Lasagna, M.D., known as the "Sigmund Freud of Clinical Pharmacology" for having published one of the first scientific papers on the so-called "placebo effect" in patients. (Courtesy of the Tufts Center for the Study of Drug Development)

Right: Robert Gallo, M.D., founder and director of the Institute of Human Virology who made history when he codiscovered that the HIV virus was the cause of AIDS. (Courtesy of the Institute of Human Virology)

New York that the HIV virus was the cause of AIDS. He also developed the HIV blood test, which led to a more rapid diagnosis and, is therefore, a safer blood supply for patients requiring blood transfusions. Prior to his research on AIDS, Dr. Gallo was the first to discover a human retrovirus—the T-cell virus—as one of the few viruses to cause leukemia and other cancers. Leonard J. Cerullo, M.D., founder and medical director of the Chicago Institute of Neurosurgery and Neuroresearch, is one of the top neurosurgeons in the United States. He pioneered the use of noninvasive lasers in neurosurgeries.

Anthony Fauci, M.D., is the director of the National Institute of Allergy and Infectious Diseases. An internationally renowned scientist, Dr. Fauci has been a pioneer in the research of and treatment of immune-related diseases. He has developed effective treatments for once fatal diseases such as polyarteritis nodosa and Wegener's Granulomatosis. He has made major contributions to a better understanding on how the AIDS virus destroys the body's immune system leading to deadly infections. The author or coauthor of more than one thousand scientific articles and several books, Dr. Fauci has delivered many lectures throughout the world and has garnered numerous prestigious awards, including more than twenty honorary doctorates from universities in the United States.

In 1999, Catherine D. DeAngelis, M.D., was unanimously recommended to become the editor of *The Journal of the American Medical Association* one of

Left: Catherine D. DeAngelis, M.D., the first woman editor of the Journal of American Medicine in its nearly one hundred twenty year history. (Courtesy of JAMA)

Right: Anthony S. Fauci, M.D., is the Director of the National Institute of Allergy and Infectious Disease. (Courtesy of the National Institute of Allergy and Infectious Disease)

the most prestigious medical journals in the world. She is the first woman editor of *JAMA* in its more than 120-year history. It has a circulation of nearly 400,000 in 148 countries. Another Italian-American physician, Margaret Giannini, dedicated her life to working with the physically challenged. She was a founder, and for many years the director of the Development Disabilities Center of New York Medical College, the first and now the largest facility for the developmentally disabled in the world. In 2002, Dr. Giannini was appointed director of the Office of Health and Disability of the U. S. Department of Health and Human Services.

The Italian-American contributions to the visual arts have been enormous, representing every mode, style, and school of painting and sculpture. Among those Italian-American painters who painted in the classical style are Constantino Brumidi, Albert Operti, Eugenio Latilla, Fabrino Julio, Joseph Pagnani Nicholas Romano, and Donatus

138

Left: Louis O. Guglielmo's "View in Chambers Street," 1936. (Courtesy of Newark Museum Collection)

Below: "The Fourteenth Station" by Pietro Montana which is one of his "Stations of the Cross" in the War Memorial Chapel at Fordham University. (Courtesy of Fordham University)

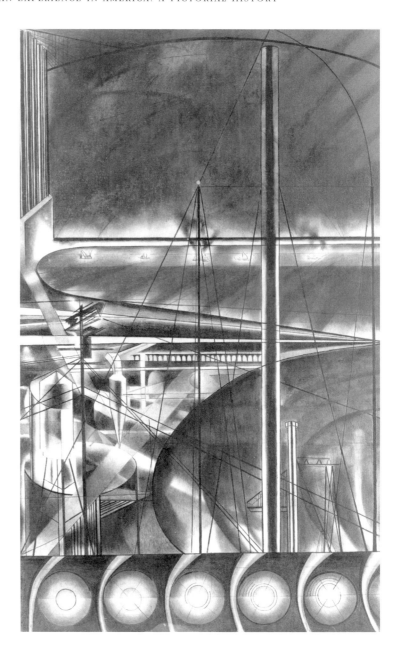

**Joseph Stella's "The Port,"
1922 from his "New York
Interpreted." (Courtesy of the
Newark Museum Collection)**

Buonngiorno, whereas modern painters include Joseph Stella, Louis Guglielmo, Peppino Mangravite, Attilio Salemni, Nicholas Marsicano, and Paul Pollaro. The overwhelming majority of statues, monuments, and memorials in America have been sculpted by Italians and Italian-Americans. Attilio Piccirilli and his brothers sculpted some of the most impressive monuments in the country, the battleship Maine in New York's Central Park, and the carving of Chester French's sculpture of the statute of Abraham Lincoln for the Lincoln Memorial in Washington, D.C., Gaetano Russo sculpted the Columbus Monument at Columbus Circle in New York, and Pasquale Civiletti's life-size

**"Girl Combing Her Hair"
by Peppino Mangravite.
(Courtesy of the
Pennsylvania Academy
of Fine Arts)**

statue of Giuseppe Verdi dominates Verdi Square in New York City. Monuments by Anthony De Francisci, Gaetano Cecere, Beniamino Bufano, Conrad Marcarelli, and Pietro Montana can be found from New York to California. Nicola D'Ascenzo's craftmanship in the art of stained glass and mosaics can be seen in such buildings as the Folger Shakespeare Library in Washington, D.C., and the Cathedral of St. John the Divine in New York City. The leading Italian-American architect in the United States is Pietro Belluschi, who designed more than one thousand buildings in this country during his near half-century career.

A good many of the literary works written by Italian immigrants and their descendants have related the agonies and joys of the Italian experience in America. For example, Pietro Di Donato's best selling novel, *Christ in Concrete*, recounts the trials, tribulations, and sufferings of an Italian immigrant family trying to escape from the

Daniel Chester French's sculpture of Lincoln carved by Attilio Piccirilli which is in the "Lincoln Memorial" in Washington D.C. (Courtesy of the Library of Congress)

Attilio Piccirilli's sculpture of the "Battleship Maine" in New York's Central Park. (Courtesy of the New York Historical Society)

The craftsmanship of Nicola D'Ascenzo as shown in his stained glass creation in the Folger Library in Washington D.C. (Courtesy of the Folger Shakespeare Library)

Above: Pietro Belluschi, architect who designed more that 1000 major buildings in America. (Courtesy of Pietro Belluschi)

Right: The Equitable Building in Portland, Oregon, designed by Pietro Belluschi. (Courtesy of Pietro Belluschi)

The Julliard School of Music at Lincoln Center in New York designed by Pietro Belluschi. (Courtesy of Pietro Belluschi)

143

Arturo Giovannitti, whose poems in *Arrows in the Gale* present a deep and powerful insight into the social, economic and political problems of American society in the first decades of the twentieth century. (Courtesy of the Archives of Labor and urban Affairs, Wayne State University)

Helen Barolini is one of the most prolific Italian-American writers. Her poems, essays and novels have created a bridge between the United States, her homeland, and Italy, the ancestral land. (Courtesy of Helen Barolini)

Jerre Mangione is the author of a dozen books of fiction and non-fiction, including the best selling memoirs *Mount Allegro*. (Courtesy of NIAF)

slum conditions of their Little Italy. Similarly, John Fante's *Wait Until Spring, Bandini* tells the story of Svevo Bandini, a construction worker who works only seasonally, and the poverty his family must endure when he is unemployed during the greater part of the year. On the other hand, Jerre Mangione's novel *Mount Allegro* captivates his readers by telling a warm and moving story of his Sicilian immigrant family caught between the culture of their native Sicily and life in their newly adopted country, the United States. Mangione also coauthored with Ben Morreale the critically acclaimed *La Storia: Five Centuries of the Italian-American Experience*. In *The Paesanos*, author Jo Pagano reminisces—in almost comic fashion—about growing up in America surrounded by the environment of the culture and lifestyle of his Italian immigrants family. Other Italian-American authors who have described various aspects of the Italian experience in America are Michael de Capete, Guido d'Agostino, Emilio Gardilla, and Garibaldi La Polla.

Two Italian-American authors who have enjoyed tremendous success in America are Mario Puzo and Gay Talese. Puzo, the product of a Neapolitan ghetto in New York's Lower East Side, has developed into one of the most talented and popular novelists and screenplay writers in contemporary America. Author of a number of outstanding novels including *The Fortunate Pilgrim*, *Fools Die*, and *Inside Las Vegas*, Puzo is best known for *The Godfather*. This best selling novel was made into a movie which has become one of the highest-grossing films in the history of the American cinema. Puzo, who wrote the screenplay for *The Godfather*, also wrote the screenplay for *The Godfather II*, *Earthquake*, *Superman*, and *Superman II*. Equally successful as a novelist is Gay Talese, known for his exhaustive research and elegant style. His most recent best-seller, *Unto the Sons*, is an historical memoir about Italian immigration to America. Among his other best-sellers are *Honor Thy Father*, a novel supposedly based on the life of Mafia chieftain Joe Bonanno, *Thy Neighbor's Wife*, and *Kingdom and the Power*. Another outstanding contemporary author, Don De Lillo, has published novels, plays, and short stories. His critically acclaimed books include *Americana*, *Underworld*, *Great Jones Street*, and *White Noise*, for which he won the National Book Award.

Gay Talese, best selling author known for such works as *Honor Thy Father, Thy Neighbor's Wife,* and *Unto The Sons*. (Courtesy of the National Italian-American Foundation)

Among the most talented poets in the history of America are Italian-Americans such as Arturo Giovannitti, Emanuel Carnevali, Lawrence Ferlinghetti, and John Ciardi. Giovannitti's collected poems published under the title of *Arrows in the Gale*, and Carnavali's scattered poems on immigrant life in the 1920s present a deep and powerful insight into the social, economic, and political problems that confronted American society during the first several decades of the twentieth century. Ferlinghetti is best known as a protest poet and leader of the San Francisco movement in poetry prevalent in the 1950s and 1960s. *His Coney Island of the Mind* gained him a reputation as one of the most prominent poets in the United States. Undoubtedly one of the most brilliant poets in contemporary America is John Ciardi. His poems, books of poetry, and literary criticisms have won him dozens of prizes and honors. His long-time position as poetry editor of the *Saturday Review* has helped establish the journal as one of the leading literary magazines in the country. Dana Gioia is an internationally acclaimed poet, critic, and translator of poetry. His *Interrogations at Noon*, a collection of poems won the American Book Award in 2002. He is a translator of poetry, publishing a translation of Seneca's *The Madness of*

John Ciardi, poet and longtime literary editor of *Saturday Review*. (Courtesy of John Ciardi)

146

Hercules, which was performed by the Verse Theater in Manhattan. Gioia, an influential critic, is best known for his book *Can Poetry Matter?* In 2003 President George W. Bush named him chairman of the National Endowment for the Arts.

Thousands of Italian-Americans are employed as writers, reporters, editors, commercial artists, cartoonists, photographers, and executives on hundreds of newspapers and magazines that are published throughout the country. Some serve as freelance writers and photographers, or as scriptwriters for television, radio, and film. Still others are news broadcasters, game show hosts, and disk jockeys. Tens of thousands of Italian-Americans hold teaching positions in primary schools, secondary schools, colleges, and universities. They serve as principals and chief college administrators. In every academic discipline in the arts, sciences, and humanities, Italian-Americans can be found making their special contribution to the education of America's youth.

Lawrence Ferlinghetti, poet whose numerous books of poetry including *Coney Island of the Mind* and *Open Eye, Open Heart*, have gained him an international reputation. (Photo by George Hoffman— Courtesy of New Directions Publishing Corp.)

Only in recent decades, however, are Americans becoming more aware of the enormous contributions that Italian-Americans have made to American life. The credit for this better understanding of the Italian contribution belongs, to a great extent, to the splendid accomplishments of the num-

Dana Gioia is an internationally known poet, critic, educator, and former business executive who is presently serving as Chairman of the National Endowment for the Arts. (Courtesy of the National Endowment for the Arts)

Above left: Giovanni Schiavo, the "Dean of Italian-American Historians," who authored more than twenty books and numerous articles on Italian experience in America. (Courtesy of Giovanni Schiavo)

Above right: John Cuneo, Sr., the founder of Cuneo Press which became one of the largest and most successful publishing businesses in the United States. (Courtesy of John Cuneo, Jr.)

The National Italian-American Foundation headquarters in Washington, D.C. (Courtesy of NIAF)

Left: Vincenzo Sellaro, M.D., founder of the Sons of Italy in New York City on June 22, 1905. (Courtesy of the Order Sons of Italy, Courtesy of Sons of Italy)

Right: Dr. Anthony P. Vastola, who founded the first chapter of UNICO in Waterbury, Connecticut in 1922. (Courtesy of UNICO National)

ber of Italian-Americans in every occupation and in every community throughout the United States. It is also due to the scholars in the humanities and social sciences who have researched and published their studies on the Italian experience in America. In this regard, top honors must go to Italian-American historians, especially to Giovanni Schiavo, Dominic Candeloro, Philip Cannistraro, Roy P. Domenico, Virginia Yans-McLaughlin, Lawrence F. Pisani, Alexander De Conde, Andre F. Rolle, Humbert S. Nelli, Luciano Iorizzo, Salvatore Mondello, Francis A.J. Ianni, Rudolph Vecoli, Silvano and Lydio Tomasi, Salvatore La Gumina, Richard Gambino, and Francesco Cordasco.

Of the more than one thousand six hundred estimated Italian-American organizations in the Untied States, the National Italian-American Foundation (NIAF), the Order Sons of Italy in America (OSIA), and UNICO are among the largest and most active in promoting cultural, social, and educational programs, and presenting a positive image of Italian-Americans.

The National Italian-American Foundation is the major advocate in Washington, D.C., for the nation's twenty-five million Italian-Americans. Its mission is to preserve and protect Italian-American heritage and culture. Through its many programs, the

President Bush at the White House signing the 2002 Columbus Day proclamation. The President of the Sons of Italy, Robert Messa, is at the extreme right. (Courtesy of Sons of Italy)

Below: A Sons of Italy class, circa 1915. Here immigrants learned English and were encouraged to become U.S. Citizens (Courtesy of Sons of Italy)

NIAF helps young Italian-Americans with their education and careers, works closely with Congress and the White House to promote the appointment of Italian-Americans in government, encourages the teaching of Italian language and culture in U. S. schools, monitors the portrayal of Italian-Americans by the news and entertainment industries, and strengthens cultural and economic ties between Italy and the United States. Every year, the NIAF honors outstanding Italians and Italian-Americans at its anniversary gala dinner, an event that draws nearly three thousand people from the United States and abroad to Washington, D.C.

The UNICO logo. (Courtesy of UNICO National)

Founded in 1905 by Dr. Vincenzo Sellaro in New York City as a mutual-aid society for Italian immigrants, the OSIA is the longest established and largest organization

Group of UNICO National Officers in front of the National Float that is part of a large contingent that UNICO has marching in the New York City Parade each Columbus Day for over 20 years. (Courtesy of UNICO National)

UNICO Scranton Chapter members at its Soccer Cup Fund Raiser 2004 presenting check to the "Jimmy V (Valvano) Foundation" for Cancer Research. (Courtesy of UNICO Scranton Chapter)

for men and women of Italian heritage in the United States. Headquartered in Washington, D.C., OSIA today has more than six hundred thousand members and supporters and a network of more than seven hundred chapters throughout the United States, making it the leading service and advocacy organization for Italian-Americans. As part of its mission OSIA encourages the study of the Italian language and culture in schools and universities and promotes Italian-American history, culture, and traditions. Through the Sons of Italy Foundation, established in 1959, it has given tens of millions of dollars to scholarships, medical research, disaster relief, and other projects. The Order Sons of Italy in America's commission for social justice is committed to fighting racism, prejudice, and defamation not only against Italian-Americans but also against all ethnic groups, races, religions, and cultures.

UNICO was founded by Dr. Anthony P. Vastola and a small group of men in Waterbery, Connecticut, in 1922. Today, under the leadership of UNICO National, with headquarters in Bloomfield, New Jersey, it has become a nationwide service organization whose membership is open to American men and women of Italian heritage, or

persons married to men and women of Italian heritage, of good character and reputation. It encourages its memberships, numbering about ten thousand, to promote actively their cultural heritage within the general community. Through its local chapters, the largest of which is located in Scranton, Pennsylvania, it conducts a wide range of activities in awarding scholarships, fighting defamation, and conducting a variety of charity, health, and service programs.

Casa Italiana at Columbia University. (Courtesy of the Columbian Collection at Columbia University in New York)

Other organizations such as the American-Italian Historical Association collects, preserves, studies, and publishes articles, books, and journals on the American past in the United States and Canada. The Casa Italiana of Columbia University is a resource on Italian culture for both the university and the broader community sponsoring lectures, exhibits, and other events depicting various aspects of Italian culture, literature, and language. While the America-Italy Society offers courses in Italian literature, language, and cooking, and sponsors lectures, films, concerts, and social events stressing the cultural link between Italy and the United States, the Italian-American Cultural Society aims to preserve Italian heritage and to publicize Italian-American contributions in the United States, Italy, and the world. All of these leading institutions and organizations have become indispensible in their assistance to scholars and laymen in gaining a fundamental insight into Italian-American history and culture.

BIBLIOGRAPHICAL
SOURCES

Amfitheatrof, Erik. *Children of Columbus: An Informal History of the Italians in the New World*. Boston: Little, Brown and Company, 1973.

Brownstone, David M., et al. *Island of Hope, Island of Tears*. New York: Rawson, Wade Publishers, Inc., 1979.

Cannistraro, Philip and Meyer, Gerald (eds). *The Lost World of Italian American Radicalism*. New York: Praeger, 2003.

Chandler, David Leon. *Brothers in Blood: The Rise of the Criminal Brotherhoods*. New York: E.P. Dutton And Co., Inc., 1975.

Cordasco, Francesco, and Bucchioni, Eugene. *The Italians: Social Backgrounds of an American Group*. Clifton, New Jersey: Augustus M. Kelley, Publishers, 1974.

De Conde, Alexander. *Half Bitter, Half Sweet: An Excursion into Italian-American History*. New York: Charles Scribner's Sons, 1971.

DiStasi, Lawrence (ed) *Dream Streets: The Big Book of Italian American Culture*. New York: Harper & Row, 1989.

Domenico, Roy P. *Remaking Italy in the Twentieth Century*. Lanham, MD: Rowman & Littlefield, 2002.

Gambino, Richard. *Blood of My Blood: The Dilemma of the Italian-Americans*. New York: Doubleday and Co. Inc., 1974; reprinted., Garden City, New York: Anchor Books, 1975.

Giordano, Joseph (ed). *The Italian American Catalog*. New York: Doubleday and Co. Inc., 1986.

Hamil, Pete. *Why Sinatra Matters*. Boston: Little, Brown and Company, 1998.

Handlin, Oscar. *A Pictorial History of Immigration*. New York: Crown Publishers, Inc., 1972.

_____. *The Uprooted*. Boston: Little, Brown, 1931.

Hansen, Marcus Lee. *The Immigrant in American History*. Cambridge, MA: Harvard University Press, 1940.

Harvard Encyclopedia of American Ethnic Groups, s.v. "Italians," by Humbert S. Nelli.

Ianni, Frances A.J. and Elizabeth R. *A Family Business: Kinship and Social Control in Organized Crime*. New York: Russell Sage, 1972.

Iorizzo, Luciano J. and Mondella, Salvatore. *The Italian Americans*. Boston: Twayne Publishers, 1980.

Johnson, Colleen Leary. *Growing Up and Growing Old in Italian American Families*. New Brunswick: Rutgers University Press, 1985.

Kessner, Thomas. The Golden Door: *Italian and Jewish Immigrant Mobility in New York City 1880–1915*. New York: Oxford University Press, 1977.

La Gumina, Salvatore J. *An Album of the Italian-Americans*. New York: Franklin Watts, Inc., 1972.

La Gumina, Salvatore J. and Cavaioli, Frank J. *The Ethnic Dimension in American Society*. Boston: Holbrook Press, Inc., 1974; reprinted., Boston: Holbrook Press, Inc., 1975.

La Gumina, Salvatore J., Cavaioli, Frank, Primeggia, Joseph, and Varacalli, Joseph (eds.). *The Italian American Experience: An Encyclopedia*. New York: Garland, 1999.

Laurino, Maria. *Were You Always An Italian?: Ancestors and Other Icons of Italian America*. New York: W.W. Norton, 2000.

Lombardo, Anthony. *The Italians in America*. Chicago: Claretian Publications, 1973.

Lopreato, Joseph. *Italian Americans*. from *Ethnic Groups in Comparative Perspective*, generaled., Peter I. Rose. New York: Random House, 1970.

Lord, Eliot, et al. *The Italians in America*. New York: B.F. Buck, 1905.

Mangano, Antonio. *Sons of Italy: A Social and Religious Study of the Italians in America*. New York: Russell and Russell, 1917.

Mangione, Jerre. *America Is Also Italian*. New York: G.P. Putnam's Sons, 1969.

Mangione, Jerre and Morreale, Ben. *La Storia: Five Centuries of the Italian American Experience*. New York: Harper-Collins, 1992.

Marinacci, Barbara. *They Came From Italy*. New York: Dodd, Mead Co., 1967.

Moquin, Wayne and Van Doren, Charles. *A Documentary History of the Italian Americans*. New York: Praeger Publishers, 1973.

Morreale, Ben and Carola, Robert. *Italian Americans: The Immigrant Experience*. New York: Beaux Arts Editions, 2000.

Musmanno, Michael A. *The Story of the Italians in America*. Garden City, New York: Doubleday and Co., Inc., 1965.

Nelli, Humbert S. *Italians in Chicago 1880–1930: A Study in Ethnic Mobility*. New York: Oxford University Press, 1973.

Novotny, Ann. *Strangers at the Door: Ellis Island, Castle Garden, and the Great Migration to America*. Riverside, CT: The Chatham Press, Inc., 1971.

Pisani, Lawrence Frank. *The Italian in America: A Social Study and History*. New York: Exposition Press, 1957.

Riis, Jacob A. *The Battle with the Slum*. New York: The Macmillan Co., 1902; reprin ed., Montclair, NJ: Smith Publishing Corporation, 1969.

_____. *Children of the Tenements*. New York: The Macmillan Co., 1903; reprinted., New York: The Macmillan Co., 1905.

_____. *How the Other Half Lives: Studies Among the Tenements of New York*. New York: Sagamore Press Inc., 1957.

Roberts, Peter. *The New Immigration: A Study of the Industrial and Social Life of Southeastern Europeans in America*. New York: The Macmillan Co., 1913.

Rolle, Andrew F. *The American Italians: Their History and Culture*. Belmont, CA: Wadworth Publishing Co., 1972.

_____. *The Immigrant Upraised: Italian Adventurers and Colonists in an Expanding America*. Norman, OK: University of Oklahoma Press, 1968.

Rose, Philip M. *The Italians in America*. New York: George H. Doran Co., 1922; reprinted., New York: Arno Press, 1975.

Salerno, Ralph and Tompkins, John S. *The Crime Confederation: Cosa Nostra and Allied Operations in Organized Crime*. Garden City, New York: Doubleday and Co., Inc., 1969.

Salvadori, Massimo. *A Pictorial History of the Italian People*. New York: Nelson Crown, 1972.

Scarpaci, Vincenza. *A Portrait of Italians in America*. New York: Charles Scribner's Sons, 1983.

Schiavo, Giovanni E. Philip Mazzei: *One of America's Founding Fathers*. New York: The Vigo Press, 1951.

_____. *Four Centuries of Italian American History*. New York: The Vigo Press, 1957.

_____. *Italian-American History*. 2 vol. New York: The Vigo Press, 1949.

_____. *The Italians in America Before the Civil War*. New York: The Vigo Press, 1934. Steiner, Edward A. *The Immigrant Tide: Its Ebb and Flow*. 2nd ed. New York: Fleming H. Revell Company, 1909.

_____. *On the Trail of the Immigrant*. New York: Fleming H. Revell Company, 1906. Talese, Gay (ed). *Italians in America: A Celebration*. Washington, D.C.: National Italian American Foundation, 2001.

Tomasi, Silvano M. and Engel, Madeline H., (eds). *The Italian Experience in the United States*. Staten Island, New York: Center for Migration Studies, Inc., 1970.

Tomasi, Silvano M., (ed). *Perspectives in Italian Immigration and Ethnicity*. New York: Center for Migration Studies, 1977.

Vecoli, Rudolph. *The People of New Jersey*. Princeton, NJ: Van Nostrand, 1965.

Wittke, Carl. *We Who Built America: The Saga of the Immigrant*. New York: Prentice Hall, Inc., 1939. Seventh printing.

WPA. *The Italians of New York: A Survey*. New York: Random House, 1938.

INDEX